A Philosophy of Culture

Also by Morton White

The Origin of Dewey's Instrumentalism
Social Thought in America
The Age of Analysis (ed.)
Toward Reunion in Philosophy
Religion, Politics, and the Higher Learning
The Intellectual versus the City
    (with Lucia White)
Foundations of Historical Knowledge
Science and Sentiment in America
Documents in the History of American
    Philosophy (ed.)
Pragmatism and the American Mind
The Philosophy of the American Revolution
What Is and What Ought to Be Done
Journeys to the Japanese, 1952–1979
    (with Lucia White)
Philosophy, "The Federalist", and the
    Constitution
The Question of Free Will
A Philosopher's Story

A Philosophy of Culture:
The Scope of
Holistic Pragmatism

MORTON WHITE

PRINCETON UNIVERSITY PRESS

Princeton and Oxford

Copyright © 2002 by Princeton University Press

Published by Princeton University Press, 41 William Street,

Princeton, New Jersey 08540

In the United Kingdom: Princeton University Press, 3 Market Place,

Woodstock, Oxfordshire OX20 1SY

White, Morton Gabriel, 1917–

A philosophy of culture : the case for holistic pragmatism / Morton White.

p. cm.

Includes bibliographical references and index.

ISBN 0-691-09656-2 (cloth : alk. paper)

1. Pragmatism. 2. Culture—Philosophy. 3. Holism. I. Title.

B945.W453 P48 2002

144'.3—dc21   2002023664

British Library Cataloging-in-Publication Data is available

This book has been composed in Janson

Printed on acid-free paper. ∞

www.pupress.princeton.edu

Printed in the United States of America

10 9 8 7 6 5 4 3 2 1

To Helen

Contents

Prologue

I BEGIN THIS BOOK BY MAKING SOME REMARKS ON how I came to write it, hoping that they will interest the reader and help clarify my aim in writing it. I began my serious philosophical thinking under the influence of several major currents of thought, among them the pragmatism of John Dewey and the analytic philosophy of G. E. Moore. I found Moore a persuasive advocate of the view that the philosopher should analyze extralinguistic concepts, attributes, or propositions, and arrive at truths that are analytic and not dependent on experience for their support; but I soon discovered that Moore was unsure about the notion of analysis that underlay his main philosophical efforts, because he had developed serious doubts about the idea of an analytic statement. At about the same time I came to know Nelson Goodman and W. V. Quine, who, in reaction to their mentors—C. I. Lewis in Goodman's case and Carnap in Quine's—did not seek analyses of intensional entities such as concepts, attributes, and propositions, because they thought that reference to such entities was obscure and because they had no clear notion of how their identity was to be established. Sharing these doubts, I came to think that the philosopher's task is an empirical enterprise requiring an examination of how we do and should use language rather than an effort to decompose concepts.

Soon afterward, Quine, Goodman, and I concluded that the search for an empirical criterion of synonymy and therefore of analyticity was hopeless, and that if one ever did emerge, it would make the distinction between analytic and synthetic a matter of degree. I was also encouraged in this belief by Dewey's epistemological gradualism and by the epistemological holism of the logician Alfred Tarski, who held that logical statements may be components of conjunctions tested by experience. Around the middle of the twentieth century, study of Wittgenstein's later works, with their emphasis on the need for the philosopher to recognize the many different uses of language, as well as contact with J. L. Austin reinforced my view that philosophy is primarily a study of language and led me to think that Moorean analysis of concepts was a remnant of classical rationalism from whose influence even James and Dewey did not wholly escape.

Once I had shed the vestiges of rationalism in my own thinking, I came to see more clearly that Dewey was right to claim that much of the history of philosophy had been a fruitless quest for certainty; but I also saw that even he, perhaps under the influence of logical positivism, had unconsciously participated in that quest in his later writings when he accepted something like a sharp distinction between analytic and synthetic statements in his *Logic*. At about this time I was writing a book on American social thought that focused on what I called the revolt against formalism in the work of Dewey, the jurist Holmes, and others, so I was much interested in cultural history, which was certainly an empirical discipline. Thus the two souls within my breast—the philosopher and the historian—were epistemically united. I tried to bring them together in a book on the philosophy of history, where I concentrated on the language of explanation and narration, with special attention to the roles of generalization and valuation in historical inquiry.

Soon after that I began thinking seriously about Quine's view that epistemology is a branch of psychology; this line of thought led me to believe that the philosopher may view moral thinking in a holistic way and therefore should not limit holism to thinking in natural science. From this I concluded that Quine was on the wrong track when he said, as Carnap had, that philosophy of science is philosophy enough. I also came to realize that James's psychologically oriented investigations of religious experience and Dewey's of artistic creation were philosophical even though they were not exclusively concerned with language, and I saw the error of Wittgenstein's view in his *Tractatus* that "Psychology is no nearer related to philosophy than is any other natural science."[1] This position allowed me to see that philosophy of religion, philosophy of art, philosophy of law, philosophy of history, and philosophy of politics are coordinate with the philosophy of natural science, thereby buttressing a view I had already expressed. In an essay published in the early 1950s,[2] I had observed that although there were many mansions in philosophy, the more splendid ones housed metaphysics, logic, epistemology, and ethics, which lived on a commanding hilltop, while somewhere downtown were the two-family dwellings for political philosophy and jurisprudence, the small apartments for esthetics, and the boardinghouses for philosophers of the special sciences. In reaction to this invidious ordering of the philosophical disciplines, I came to think that a more democratic division of housing should be devised, one that provided better quarters for the deprived disciplines. After I came to believe that metaphysics and epistemology were empirical disciplines, I had an even stronger reason for urging this reapportionment since I came to see more clearly that those privileged parts of philosophy could not defend their conclusions by *a priori* methods. I also came to believe that ethics may be viewed as empirical if one includes feelings of moral obligation as well as sensory experiences in the pool or flux into which the ethical believer worked a manageable structure (to use a James-like figure that Quine had once used when characterizing the purpose of science).

As I reflected on my expansive conclusion about the various branches of philosophy, I began to think that the most interesting

---

[1] Ludwig Wittgenstein, *Tractatus Logico-Philosophicus*, trans. C. K. Ogden (London, 1933), 4.1121 (p. 77).
[2] See "A Plea for an Analytic Philosophy of History," in my *Religion, Politics, and the Higher Learning* (Cambridge, Mass., 1959), p. 61.

and most fruitful products of so-called linguistic philosophy were in the philosophy of culture. This appeared to me to be illustrated in Quine's work in the philosophy of science, which he at one point called a study of a Wittgensteinian game or an institution; in Goodman's work in the philosophy of art; to some extent in Holmes's legal philosophy; and in Rawls's work in the philosophy of politics. Consequently I decided to write a critical history of recent philosophy of culture to show, among other things, how such work and my own in semantics, the philosophy of history, and ethics were part of an effort to escape the influence of classical rationalism. I saw this effort as the hallmark of a movement that included Hume and Mill; that was to some extent supported in the nineteenth century by figures I call thinkers, to distinguish them from the great philosophers who wrote about culture; that was encouraged to some extent by those I call half-hearted anti-rationalists; and that was impeded by irrationalists. Although this book is in part a historical study of the roles of reason, sensory experience, and sentiment in twentieth-century philosophy of culture, it is one in which I am mainly concerned to show why certain philosophical ideas about culture should be accepted and others rejected. Therefore, I do not hesitate to express both favorable and unfavorable opinions of some of the views I examine—all this in the interest of furthering the aims of the philosophy of culture.

However, I am not concerned to explain by reference to social circumstances why certain philosophical beliefs arose at certain times and why others succeeded them. I leave that different and difficult job to others who, I hope, will not carry it out at the expense of gliding over philosophical views and the arguments offered in their behalf. In my opinion the sociohistorical explanation of the emergence of philosophical beliefs depends on an understanding of them that can be gained only by a careful study of what philosophers have said. Philosophical beliefs are not black boxes whose historical antecedents and consequences can be discerned without knowing what is inside them; but inasmuch as the philosophical task of reporting the beliefs of a philosopher is empirical, it is not radically different from the task of historians who try to say why those beliefs arose when they arose and what their effects were on society. That is why annalists who deal with ideas would do well to study the work of analysts who work in what might be called cultural philosophy.[3] I think cultural philosophy or philosophy of culture is more inclusive than philosophy of science because the latter is a study of only one cultural institution and therefore coordinate with studies of other institutions that make up a culture or a civilization. For this reason I add a terminological point that will by now be obvious: I use the word "culture" as some have used the word "civilization"— to denote those institutions—and therefore not as some anthropologists use the term.

About a half century ago in my *Age of Analysis* (1955),[4] I said that nothing could be more important than applying the techniques of analytic philosophy to subjects in the philosophy of culture; but little did I expect that by the end of the twentieth century my hope would be realized in the work of several philosophers trained in the analytic, linguistic, and pragmatic traditions who managed to free themselves from the vestiges of rationalism in logical positivism. I think that this ironic development in the history of philosophy bodes well for its future, since it opens up new avenues for humanistic inquiry. It also shows that study of the many aspects of culture is not the exclusive preserve of muddle-heads, philosophasters, and charlatans. Indeed, the relation between sane, sound, and sober philosophy of culture and its competitors today is reminiscent of what David Hume said in the introduction to his *Treatise of Human Nature* (1739) when he compared the use of what he called experimental reason in discussions of logic, morals, criticism, and politics with that of its rivals: "Amidst all this bustle 'tis not reason, which carries

[3] See my essay "Why Annalists of Ideas Should Be Analysts of Ideas," *Georgia Review* 29 (1975): 930–47.

[4] Morton White, *The Age of Analysis: Twentieth Century Philosophers, Selected, with an Introduction and Interpretive Commentary* (Boston, 1955).

the prize, but eloquence; and no man needs ever despair of gaining proselytes to the most extravagant hypothesis, who has art enough to represent it in any favourable colours. The victory is not gained by the men at arms, who manage the pike and the sword; but by the trumpeters, drummers, and musicians of the army."[5] I would prefer to use a less military figure, but I agree with what Hume was driving at as I scan the intellectual scene today. I also agree with Hume's remark in his introduction that there is no question of philosophical importance "whose decision is not compriz'd in the science of man," and that "the only solid foundation we can give to this science itself must be laid on experience and observation."[6] Would that Hume had remembered this when he distinguished sharply between statements that are based on "experimental reasoning," and statements established by "abstract reasoning." In the present study I mention examples of this sort of inconsistency as I trace the history of the philosophy of culture from the pragmatism of James and Dewey to the holistic pragmatism that avoided such inconsistency in the latter part of the twentieth century.

I must thank J. L. Austin, Isaiah Berlin, John Dewey, Nelson Goodman, H. L. A. Hart, G. E. Moore, W. V. Quine, John Rawls, and Alfred Tarski, all of them mentors or former colleagues who have helped me form my ideas. And I salute Carnap, Duhem, Hume, James, John Stuart Mill, Peirce, Russell, and Wittgenstein as heroes of philosophy upon whose work so many of us build even when criticizing their views. I salute them not merely out of piety but because I think that holistic pragmatists should regard some of their views as parts of the philosophical heritage that they accept, reject, or revise when organizing their own sensory experiences and feelings. In keeping with my holism, I think a philosopher who reflects on scientific thinking sees it in the light of some views that he inherits from past philosophers. Neither he nor the natural scientist begins with a Lockeian *tabula rasa* or with Cartesian doubt about every

---

[5] David Hume, *A Treatise of Human Nature*, ed. L. A. Selby-Bigge (Oxford, 1888), p. xviii.
[6] Ibid., p. xx.

one of his beliefs, and so his heritage consists partly of what his philosophical predecessors have said. That is why I think it important for a philosopher to know the history of his subject, much as a physicist should know the literature of hers. Those who are ignorant of it run the risk of repeating what others before them have said, and they may find themselves arguing against straw men of their own invention and tilting against what no philosopher has ever said. The twentieth century has witnessed more than its share of studied ignorance of the writings of past philosophers, partly because of what has been called the new way of words in the twentieth century; but in my opinion we do not begin to philosophize without accepting or rejecting some of the views of some philosophers before us. That is why we do well to be familiar with the writings in which those views have been advocated.

It remains for me to thank two anonymous publisher's readers for some of their comments as well as Professor Israel Scheffler, who has sympathetically read an earlier version of the manuscript. He has made very helpful suggestions about how to improve it. I wish also to thank Ms. Julia Bernheim for her expert typing of many versions of the work and Mr. Ian Malcolm of the Princeton University Press for his encouraging interest in it.

Although an author is unwise to predict anything about future work, I make bold to say that I expect to bring out a volume in which I deal critically with the earlier history of the philosophy of culture from Descartes to the end of the nineteenth century. In it I hope to show how hard it was for philosophers and other commentators on culture to free themselves completely from the grip of classical rationalism. The present work focuses on the ideas of philosophers who have tried especially hard and have had considerable success at this seemingly endless task.

Morton White
April 2002

A Philosophy of Culture

I

Holistic Pragmatism and
the Philosophy of Culture

M Y PURPOSE IN THIS BOOK IS TO PRESENT A
philosophical discussion of the main ele-
ments of civilization or culture such as science, law, religion, politics,
art, and history, a discussion in which I expound and defend a holistic, empirical, and pragmatic approach. Around the beginning of the
twentieth century, William James and John Dewey prepared the way
for pragmatic inquiry into the elements of culture that was further
developed in the second half of the century by W. V. Quine's writings on the method of logic and the natural sciences, by Nelson
Goodman's work in the philosophy of art, by John Rawls's work in
ethics, and by my own writings in ethics and the philosophy of history. I focus on this work and also on the earlier views of Justice
Oliver Wendell Holmes in legal philosophy while illustrating what
I call holistic pragmatism.

That doctrine was succinctly formulated by Quine in his famous
1951 paper, "Two Dogmas of Empiricism," when he wrote: "Each
man is given a scientific heritage plus a continuing barrage of sensory stimulation; and the considerations which guide him in warping
his scientific heritage to fit his continuing sensory promptings are,
where rational, pragmatic."[1] In several ways, this statement is espe-

---

[1] W. V. Quine, "Two Dogmas of Empiricism," in *From a Logical Point of View: Nine Logico-
Philosophical Essays* (Cambridge, 1953), p. 46; originally published in *Philosophical Review* 60
(January 1951).

cially significant. First of all, it is about the behavior of human beings and their heritage, and is for that reason about a cultural phenomenon. Second, a scientific heritage is regarded as a conjunction of many beliefs rather than as one nonconjunctive belief, thereby indicating that the view is holistic. Third, the reference to a barrage of sensory stimulation or a flux of experience indicates the empiricism of the view. Fourth, the reference to the pragmatic warping of a scientific heritage to fit sensory promptings shows that the view is in the tradition of pragmatism. According to holistic pragmatism, scientists' warpings are carried out with concern for the elegance or simplicity of the theory they adopt and with the intention to warp the heritage conservatively—that is, by engaging in what James calls minimum modification of it and what Quine calls minimum mutilation of it.

Holistic pragmatism is primarily opposed to the doctrine of classical rationalism, which holds that we have knowledge that is not tested by experience. This opposition is illustrated in the attack on the logical positivists' distinction between analytic and synthetic statements leveled by Quine, by Alfred Tarski, by Nelson Goodman, and by myself in ways that will be amplified later. Instead of claiming, as logical positivists did, that all truths of logic are analytic because they are true by virtue of the meanings of their terms and therefore not tested by sensory experience, holistic philosophers argue that because a scientific theory is a conjunction of logical statements and statements of natural science, a scientist's sensory experience may lead him to reject even a logical component of that conjunction in an effort to make the scientific theory fit those specific sensory promptings. In addition, holistic pragmatists reject the positivists' distinction between so-called analytic statements of essential predication, such as "All men are rational animals", and so-called synthetic statements, such as "All men are featherless bipeds". Holistic pragmatists hold that this positivistic distinction rests on the obscure view that "men" is synonymous with "rational animals" but not synonymous with "featherless bipeds". Finally, holistic pragmatists maintain that statements of ontology or metaphysics—for example, the statement that there are universals such as the class of men—are also conjuncts of a holistically conceived scientific theory that is pragmatically warped to fit sensory experience.

I come now to some relations between my own views and those held by Quine. I agree with most of Quine's characterization of the way in which natural scientists warp their heritage, but I do not think as Quine does that philosophy of natural science is philosophy enough—a restrictive view that, I believe, is a remnant of the logical positivism or empiricism against which he reacted in "Two Dogmas". So while I agree with him that natural science is a cultural institution whose workings a philosopher may study, I think that the philosopher may also study other institutions, most notably morality, and I treat moral thinking holistically. I believe that our scientific heritage contains not only beliefs of logic and natural science but moral beliefs as well, since I believe that a moral judge tries to organize a flux consisting of feelings of moral obligation as well as of sensory experiences. John Rawls adopts a similar view in his work on justice; and I believe that Goodman engages in pragmatic holistic thinking in his philosophy of art and that it also goes on in the philosophy of history and the philosophy of law. In my view, we may distinguish different disciplines associated with various elements of culture on the basis of their different vocabularies and substantive statements, but not by saying that we use fundamentally different methods in supporting those statements.

A FEW HISTORICAL OBSERVATIONS WILL, I THINK, MAKE THE MOTIVATION of holistic pragmatism clearer. It is primarily a reaction against the rationalism espoused by Descartes when he said that at least some truths of natural science may be established by pure reason along with the truths of pure mathematics, by Locke when he defended the doctrine that ethics is a demonstrative science that he likened to pure mathematics, by Kant when he tried to support moral truths as necessary and *a priori*, and by Hegel in places where he seems to spin out a theory of historical development by using pure reason. And while Hume opposed Locke's rationalism in ethics and Descartes's rationalism in the philosophy of religion, as Mill did in political philosophy when he rejected the doctrine of natural rights, in my view neither Hume nor Mill went far enough in their rejection of rationalism. Hume explicitly advocated a sharp distinction between two kinds of truth much like the logical positivists' later distinction between analytic and synthetic truth, and Mill thought that attributes or concepts are analyzed when we support essential predications that, he said, correspond to what Kant calls analytic judgments.[2]

In addition to these earlier figures, a number of empirically oriented philosophers of the early twentieth century were part-time rationalists. For example, Pierre Duhem, an early advocate of holism in the philosophy of physics, accepted a sharp epistemic distinction between physical and mathematical truth. And while we shall see that Bertrand Russell once said with apparent approval that William James was what I would call a holistic pragmatist, James inconsistently maintained a sharp distinction between *a priori* and empirical truth in *Pragmatism*, and Russell himself abandoned holistic pragmatism later on. Moreover, John Dewey, in some ways the most anti-dualistic philosopher of culture in the twentieth century, also seemed to accept a distinction between two kinds of truth that was rationalistic.[3]

The philosophers I have just mentioned were not alone in succumbing to the attractions of rationalism, whether full-fledged or half-fledged. They were joined by many philosophically oriented writers on culture who are not usually associated with rationalism. For example, in the nineteenth century Ludwig Feuerbach, who

---

[2] J. S. Mill, *A System of Logic, Ratiocinative and Inductive: Being a Connected View of the Principles of Evidence, and the Methods of Scientific Investigation*, ed. J. M. Robson (Toronto, 1973), book I, chap. 6, sec. 5 (1:116 n. 62).

[3] See "Experiment and Necessity in Dewey's Philosophy," in my *Pragmatism and the American Mind: Essays and Reviews in Philosophy and Intellectual History* (New York, 1973), pp. 138–54.

called himself an anthropologist of religion, claimed to have discovered the essence of Christianity by a method that is rationalistic, and Friedrich Nietzsche, also a critic of rationalism, claimed to know the essence of life and value. A Marxist like Friedrich Engels thought—whether with Marx's approval is not clear—he could deduce a philosophy of history—historical materialism—from dialectical materialism, thereby trying to do for history what Descartes tried to do for physics and Locke tried to do for ethics.

It is an irony of intellectual history that many of the half-rationalists I have mentioned were psychologists or social scientists who might have been expected to reject rationalism root and branch. Hume was a psychologist and historian; Mill was an economist and political theorist; many Marxists have been economists or historians; Nietzsche called himself a psychologist; and James and Dewey wrote books devoted to psychology. Most of them were empirically oriented humanists in the broad sense of that term, waving the anti-rationalistic banners of romanticism, positivism, materialism, and pragmatism and yet reserving a role for pure, nonempirical reason in their thinking. The irony of their being half-rationalists helps explain why it took twentieth-century philosophers so long to escape the influence of what Dewey called "the quest for certainty," an irony that was increased by the fact that he seems to have taken part in that quest. The emergence of a thoroughgoing holistic pragmatism was impeded not only by wide acceptance of Cartesian rationalism and half-rationalism, but also by wide acceptance in the twentieth century of views on *a priori* knowledge held by the analytic philosophers Bertrand Russell, G. E. Moore, C. I. Lewis, and Rudolf Carnap. All of these distinguished philosophers accepted versions of the distinction between analytic and synthetic statements, though Moore voiced doubts about its clarity toward the end of his life.

In concluding this introductory chapter, I want to say a few words about how one may move from the view that philosophy of science is philosophy enough to the view that philosophy is philosophy of culture. If epistemology is in great measure a descriptive psychological account of the cultural institution of scientific thinking that leads epistemologists to promulgate a rule governing it, we may say that they give a descriptive and a normative account of moral thinking. While the natural scientist tries to work a manageable structure into a flux of sensory experience, I believe the moralist tries to work a manageable structure into a flux composed of both sensory experiences and feelings of moral obligation. And while doing so, the moralist may warp her heritage—which includes moral statements as well as logical statements and factual statements that she believes with different degrees of confidence—to fit her sensory and emotional promptings. I think Rawls does something like this when he seeks to arrive at what he calls reflective equilibrium; certainly Goodman does when he moves back and forth from rules of inference to accepted inferences in an effort to arrive at such equilibrium. We shall also see that when Goodman abandons the question "What is the essence of art?" for the question "What are the symptoms of art?" he treats philosophy of art as an empirical inquiry. So, once we regard the philosophy of science as the philosophy of one element of culture, we may say that there are other elements of culture that may be studied from a holistic, empirical, and pragmatic point of view. In the next two chapters I begin by discussing the views of James on religion and those of Dewey on art; for in spite of their occasional lapses into rationalism, they are progenitors of more recent efforts to broaden the scope of philosophy from an examination of logic and physics to an empirical examination of other elements of civilization or culture.

II

William James

Psychologist and Philosopher of Religion

WILLIAM JAMES AND JOHN DEWEY WERE THE first and foremost twentieth-century American philosophers of culture. When James wrote on religion and Dewey on art, they prepared the way for later philosophers who treated religion, art, science, law, history, and politics empirically. They held that philosophy is a capacious discipline that goes beyond the philosophy of science, and they tried—not always successfully—to surrender the idea that philosophical truth is arrived at by the analysis of abstract entities such as attributes and propositions. Although James and Dewey adumbrated a philosophy that completely rejected rationalism, they did not reach one. That was left to philosophers who explicitly adopted holistic pragmatism, who rejected the Humeian dichotomy between logico-mathematical and empirical truth, and who abandoned the Cartesian idea that philosophy extracts the essence of mind, of body, of truth, of the good, and of the beautiful.

James on Religious Experience

I begin by considering the views of James on what he called religious experience, and in the next section I discuss what may be called his methodological monism. He encouraged other philosophers to use empirical methods; but unlike many of them, he held that religious belief is grounded in experience because he thought experience included mystical feelings as well as the data of the five standard senses. In his *Varieties of Religious Experience*, which was delivered as a set of lectures in 1901 and 1902, James deliberately set himself against treating religion as an institutional, corporate, or tribal product and said he was concerned with the religious experience as it lives itself out within the private breast.[1] Not only did he avoid the study of ecclesiastical institutions, he held that the baseness commonly charged to religion's account is almost entirely due to what he called religion's practical partner, the spirit of corporate dominion, and that the bigotries of religion are chargeable to what he called religion's wicked intellectual partner, the spirit of dogmatic dominion, or the passion for laying down the law in an absolutely closed-in theoretic system (p. 271). James insisted on separating religion as he conceived it from organized religion's hatred of nonconforming individuals—from its baiting of Jews, its hunting of Albigenses, its murdering of Mormons, and its massacring of Armenians—identifying it instead with feelings that he called good to live by and strength-giving (p. 271).

When James focused on the religious beliefs of individuals, he did so with a psychologist's interest in their origins and a philosopher's interest in their truth and grounds. Unlike Freud among his contemporaries in psychology, he carried out his investigations of religious beliefs while adopting a sympathetic attitude toward religious believers. Whereas Freud in *The Future of an Illusion* (1928) avoided serious discussion of whether religious doctrines are true or false, James openly defended religious supernaturalism while rejecting the theological rationalism, the Deism, and the skepticism represented by the different characters in Hume's *Dialogues Concerning Natural Religion*. Like Hume, James rejected scholastic and Cartesian proofs of the existence of God, as well as the argument from design, but as

---

[1] William James, *The Varieties of Religious Experience* (Cambridge, Mass., 1985), pp. 13, 269. This edition is hereafter cited parenthetically in the text.

an admirer of Darwin's work he had even more reason than Hume to reject the latter argument. Though he called himself an empiricist and a pragmatist, James was bent on rehabilitating the element of feeling in religion and subordinating its intellectual part (p. 345).

Feeling figured in the *Varieties* both as a philosophical avenue to theological truth and as a subject of psychological inquiry. James said it was by feeling that his religious informants—his saints and mystics—arrived at their beliefs in an unseen order; and although he admitted he was unable to feel what they felt, he said he relied on their reports of their feelings much as he relied on the reports of scientific experts who told him what they saw and what he did not see. James vividly described those feelings or emotions in the *Varieties*, where he portrayed the trances, automatisms, and dreams of his informants with the help of fascinating documents that make up a large part of the work. He said that his subjects had their religious feelings because they were influenced by a supernatural being with whom they were in contact through "the doorway" of their subliminal or subconscious selves. James believed that God inspired the religious feelings of those he called religious geniuses, but he also said that *the reason* why he believed that God exists is that those geniuses felt "an objective presence" and that he trusted their reports as he trusted those of authorities in science; he added, moreover, that a belief in God was "good for living," thereby anticipating his pragmatic theory of truth. His view of the relationship between the religious saint's feeling and the saint's belief in God resembled that of the psychologist who says that looking at a piece of paper causes her to have a sensation of white *and* that of the philosopher who says that his having that sensation constitutes a reason for his belief that there is a white object before him. When James characterized religious experience, he said that there is a uniform deliverance among men in which religions all appear to meet, a deliverance that is made up of two parts. The first is the belief that there is a feeling of uneasiness—"a sense that there is *something wrong* about us as we naturally stand." And the second is the belief that *"we are saved from the wrongness* by making proper connexion with the higher powers" (p. 400). James held that the second belief implies that there is a larger universe that includes the physical world as well as an unseen spiritual order; that our true end in life is union with that higher spiritual order; and that during prayer and communion with it, energy flows so as to produce effects in the phenomenal world (p. 382).

When James tried to explain religious feelings by saying they were caused by the Deity entering the minds of religious geniuses through their subconscious selves, his forthright critic James Leuba pointed out that although James was well aware that psychologists thought these feelings were of purely subjective origin and therefore could be explained without appealing to a supernatural God, James was not content with that naturalistic explanation. Although James called the discovery of the subconscious the most important discovery of psychology during the forty years before his *Varieties* appeared, Leuba complained that he regarded the naturalistic explanation of religious feelings advanced by scientific psychologists as unsatisfactory because he preferred to explain religious feeling by referring to an extrahuman personality. Why, Leuba asked, was James not satisfied with the purely naturalistic theory of the subconscious self that had so successfully explained the phenomena of multiple personality, psychic manifestations of hysteria, and other nervous disorders? Why did James use a supernatural hypothesis to explain the purely subjective experiences that his religious informants had? Because, Leuba said without mincing words, James did not *want* to help out science as Leuba conceived it: "Psychologist turned metaphysician, his interest now lies in a ground of explanation which, as Kant says, 'lifts us above the necessity of investigating nature.' "[2] In order to reinforce his attack, Leuba quoted James's statement about the success of psychologists in using the naturalistic theory of a subliminal

---

[2] James A. Leuba, "Professor William James's Interpretation of Religious Experience," *International Journal of Ethics* 14 (1903–04): 326.

self to explain hallucinations, pains, convulsions, and paralyses of feeling and of motion, as well as the symptoms of hysteria. But then he pinpointed James's retreat from naturalism by quoting James's remark that if an orthodox Christian were to ask him whether his reference to a subliminal self excluded the direct presence of the Deity altogether, he, James, would have to say frankly that he did not see why it necessarily should (*Varieties*, p. 197).

James argued that we can explain ordinary sense perception without appealing to the power of God, but that "just as our primary wide-awake consciousness throws open our senses to the touch of things material, so it is logically conceivable that *if there be* higher spiritual agencies that can directly touch us, the psychological condition of their doing so *might be* our possession of a subconscious region which alone should yield access to them. The hubbub of the waking life might close a door which in the dreamy Subliminal might remain ajar or open" (p. 197). But here Leuba reminded him of his concessions to naturalism when describing the effect of alcohol and nitrous oxide. James had said that "the sway of alcohol over mankind is unquestionably due to its power to stimulate the mystical faculties of human nature, usually crushed to earth by the cold facts and dry criticisms of the sober hour"; that "the drunken consciousness is one bit of the mystic consciousness"; and that "nitrous oxide and ether, especially nitrous oxide, when sufficiently diluted with air, stimulate the mystical consciousness in an extraordinary degree" (p. 307). Such statements by James, his critic said, seemed to explain mystical consciousness by referring to a natural cause—but James was not satisfied with that explanation. Instead, James concluded on the basis of his personal experiments with nitrous oxide that it induces a form of consciousness that makes possible a kind of metaphysical insight: "It is as if the opposites of the world, whose contradictoriness and conflict make all our difficulties, were melted into unity. Not only do they, as contrasted species, belong to one and the same genus, but *one of the species*, the nobler and the better one, *is itself the genus, and so soaks up and absorbs its opposite into itself.*" This, James admitted, was a "dark saying . . . when thus expressed in terms of common logic," but he could not "wholly escape from its authority." He felt "as if it must mean something, something like what the Hegelian philosophy means, if one could only lay hold of it more clearly. Those who have ears to hear, let them hear; to me the living sense of its reality only comes in the artificial mystic state of mind" (p. 308).

Veering from the jocose anti-Hegelianism he had expressed in his earlier article "On Some Hegelisms" (1882), James said in his *Varieties* that the insights he had gained under the influence of nitrous oxide showed that "our normal waking consciousness, rational consciousness as we call it, is but one special type of consciousness, whilst all about it, parted from it by the filmiest of screens, there lie potential forms of consciousness entirely different" (pp. 307–8). James did not conclude that he was hallucinating or having delusions rather than true metaphysical insights after sniffing nitrous oxide. On the contrary, James thought his visions under its influence came through an avenue to religious truth that differs from our ordinary senses, and that some men, like his saints, can arrive at such truths *without* taking drugs. When James tried his hardest to persuade his audience of this, he scaled down his theological claim by not going beyond the statement that such a mystical avenue to truth *may* exist, by saying that a mystic had a *right* (as distinct from a duty) to believe that it existed as well as a *right* to believe truths entered his consciousness through this avenue. And when James replied in a letter to Leuba's animadversions, he scaled down his thesis even further, saying, "Of course, the 'subliminal' theory is an inessential hypothesis."[3] In other words, James was willing to abandon the idea of a subliminal "doorway" through which God's energy and his support flowed to those who believed in him. Jetti-

---

[3] In Ralph Barton Perry, *The Thought and Character of William James, as Revealed in Unpublished Correspondence and Notes, together with His Published Writings* (Boston, 1935), 2:351.

soning the idea that God caused the saints' religious feelings by acting through this doorway, James defended his supernaturalism by declaring that large numbers of the best men in their best moments shared a feeling of unseen reality, that he himself responded with agreement in his deep moments to the utterances of such men, and that the belief in God which it supported was good for the purposes of living. James said it was preposterous to suppose that the feeling of the religious genius or saint should be held to carry no objective significance, and especially preposterous if that feeling combined harmoniously with what he called our otherwise grounded philosophy of objective truth.

In his reply to the critical Leuba, James repeated what he had said in the *Varieties* about his having no living sense of commerce with a God, and added that he envied those who did have such commerce with him. He admitted that he was devoid of "*Gottesbewusstein* in the directer and stronger sense," but declared that something in him responded when he heard utterances from that quarter issued by others. He said he recognized the deeper voice, and that something told him "*thither lies truth*." Though raised as a Christian, he vehemently insisted that he had outgrown Christianity and that its entanglement in any mystical utterance had to be removed and overcome before he could even take such an utterance seriously. He said, however, that he harbored a "mystical germ," a "very common germ" that creates the rank and file of believers and withstands all purely atheistic criticism.[4] This reference in his reply to the rank and file of believers echoed his remark in the *Varieties* that mankind instinctively believed that God is real (p. 407), but at other points in that work he said it was vain for the rationalistic majority to grumble when mystics say they have been "there" and know the truth. He countered such grumbling by claiming that the majority's scientific beliefs are based on evidence exactly similar in nature to the evi-

---

[4] Ibid., pp. 350–51.

dence offered by mystics for theirs. The five senses of that majority assure them of certain facts, James asserted, but mystical experiences are as direct perceptions of fact for those who have them as any sensations are for the majority (p. 336).

Although James sometimes said that belief in God was an instinctive belief of all mankind and sometimes said that it was a belief of a minority, his fundamental point was that we cannot establish or refute the claim that there is a mystical consciousness merely by polling individuals. Even if most scientists were to deny that we can have veridical experiences of an unseen order, their denial would cut no ice for James. He maintained stoutly that the mystic could accuse the anti-mystic of religious blindness if the latter said he did not feel the objective presence that the mystic felt, just as a scientist might level a similar charge against those who said they did not see what the scientist saw in her laboratory or through a telescope. James insisted that he was an empiricist; but Leuba insisted just as strongly that James was not, because Leuba identified empiricism with the view that claims to knowledge can be supported only by appealing to the normal five senses, whereas James's empiricism allowed for confirmation by mystical feeling *and* by those five senses. James maintained that just as the foundation of what he called "natural" knowledge is sensation—which, he said, is caused by the immediate nonrational influence of body on body—so there *might be* a similar direct influence from God, and our religious knowledge might be partly founded on that. He held that insofar as such feelings of influence did not clash with normal empirical evidence, the hypothesis that God exerted this influence might be corroborated.

James's idea that corroborative religious feelings harmonized with evidence of the normal senses was in keeping with the holistic intimations of what he said a few years later in his *Pragmatism*, first delivered as lectures in 1906. There he spoke of a tree trunk composed of scientific beliefs, a trunk upon which new scientific beliefs may be grafted when new sensory experiences or new desires must

be accommodated by science; and in the *Varieties* he said in effect
that we can graft the hypothesis that God exists onto a trunk containing a scientific theory like that of the subliminal self, and that
the result of such grafting can be confirmed by sense experience *and*,
as he wrote to Leuba, by the feelings of the best persons in their
best moments.[5] James conceded to Leuba that his theory that certain
persons made contact with the Deity through the doorway of the
subconscious or subliminal self was "an inessential hypothesis," but
he continued to insist that God may have caused the feelings of such
individuals as George Fox, St. Paul, and St. Teresa, just as looking
at a piece of paper causes an ordinary observer to have a sensation
of white. For James, the counterpart of the scientist's *confirming* her
belief that the paper is white by citing a sensory experience of a
white patch is the ability of certain *feelings of the saint* to confirm his
belief in the existence of God. Very much like the Savoyard priest
in Rousseau's *Emile*, James said that scientifically oriented critics can
challenge a religious genius for proofs and put him down with
words, but they will not convince him if his "dumb intuitions" or
feelings are opposed to the critic's conclusions. Such intuitions,
James said, come from a deeper level of the self and "must be truer
than any logic-chopping rationalistic talk, however clever, that may
contradict it" (*Varieties*, p. 67).

Feeling therefore enters James's philosophy of religion in the *Varieties* at two different points. He thought that the religious feelings of
saints are brought about by God and are properly adduced by them
as evidence for their belief in God's existence, but he also thought
that the feeling of a saint that is caused by God differs from the feeling
of moral helpfulness that accompanies the saint's belief in God. According to James, a saint may validly infer "God exists" from a statement like "I feel an objective presence," or from "I sense an unseen
reality"—in which case the saint's feeling or sensing supplies him with

[5] Ibid.,pp. 334, 349.

a *direct* justification of his belief in God's existence—but the feeling of moral helpfulness of which James spoke is a feeling *about the belief* that God exists, a feeling that may be experienced not only by the saint but also by a person like James, who was not able to feel God's presence directly. This feeling of moral helpfulness may accompany the saint's belief in God even though the saint does not need that extra justification for his belief, but a nonsaint like James *did* need that extra justification. In defending his own religious belief, James thus said that the feeling of unseen reality, which *he* did not have, was not only shared by large numbers of men in their best moments but was good for living. That was why James thought that feeling carried what he called objective significance and why he thought that in dismissing that feeling of unseen reality as a purely subjective affection, his critic Leuba opened up "the whole subject of what the word 'truth' means." James added, in anticipation of what he was to say in *Pragmatism*, that "if inferences from 'good for life' to 'true' were on principle forbidden, not religion but the whole notion of truth would probably have to be the thing overhauled and revised."[6]

The whole notion of truth and its connection with goodness for life greatly occupied James in the years after the *Varieties* and *Pragmatism* appeared, even when he treated it without exclusive attention to religious belief. But when his pragmatic views on truth were attacked by the philosophical analysts Bertrand Russell and G. E. Moore in the early years of the twentieth century, they did not focus exclusively on religious truth. Instead, they considered the general question of whether the predicate "true" is synonymous with expressions such as "useful", "good for life", or "morally helpful" in contexts that are not religious. Russell and Moore attacked James for failing to distinguish between giving a synonym for the word "true" and presenting a criterion like goodness for life by which to determine whether a belief is true. Russell said that when we ask "What does such and such a word mean?" what we want to know is "What is in the mind of a person

[6] Ibid., p. 350.

using the word?" We expect a dictionary or a philosopher to help us find the answer to this question, Russell said, but we are not given that answer when we are told only of a lawful or causal connection between truth and another property of the belief such as its usefulness.[7] Being listed in the catalogue of a library may be a criterion of whether a book is in that library or a sign that it is, Russell said, but when we say that *Moby-Dick* is in the library we do not *mean* that it is listed in the catalogue but rather that it is on a shelf. Analogously, when we say that a belief is true, we do not *mean* that it is useful even if it *is* useful. Indeed, Russell went further and said that a direct effort to find out whether a belief is true may be easier than the indirect one of finding out whether it is useful.

James replied to this sort of criticism in chapter 14 of *The Meaning of Truth*, which was titled "Two English Critics" (viz., Russell and Moore), but that is not one of James's more lucid productions. However, it does make clear that James was not interested in presenting a synonym for the word "true", and not even interested in presenting what Russell called a criterion. James writes:

> Good consequences are not proposed by us merely as a sure sign, mark, or criterion, by which truth's presence is habitually ascertained, tho they may indeed serve on occasion as such a sign; they are proposed rather as the lurking *motive* inside of every truth-claim, whether the "trower" be conscious of such motive, or whether he obey it blindly. They are proposed as the *causa existendi* of our beliefs, not as their logical cue or premise, and still less as their objective deliverance or content. They assign the only intelligible practical *meaning* to that difference in our beliefs which our habit of calling them true or false comports. No truth-claimer except the pragmatist himself need ever be aware of the part played in his own mind by consequences, and he himself is aware of it only abstractly and in general, and may at any moment be quite oblivious of it with respect to his own beliefs.[8]

---

[7] Bertrand Russell, *Philosophical Essays* (London, 1910), p. 109.
[8] William James, *The Meaning of Truth* (Cambridge, Mass., 1975), pp. 146–47.

This passage, which I do not fully understand but which James's biographer Gerald Myers regards as an important indicator of his intent,[9] shows that James was not concerned, as a Mooreian or Russellian analyst would be, to present an attribute of beliefs that is identical with that of being true. It shows, according to Myers, that James did not hold that "true" and "has good consequences" are synonymous expressions in spite of many remarks in *Pragmatism* which seemed to say just that. James saw himself as an inquirer into the motives of trowers or truth-claimers, an inquirer into the causes of their beliefs, just as he saw himself as an inquirer into the sources or causes of religious feelings in the *Varieties*. This tendency to seek the causes of belief was evident in his early essay "The Sentiment of Rationality," where he asked why we adopt our philosophical beliefs and answered as follows:

> Pretend what we may, the whole man within us is at work when we form our philosophical opinions. Intellect, will, taste, and passion cooperate just as they do in practical affairs; and lucky it is if the passion be not something as petty as a love of personal conquest over the philosopher across the way. The absurd abstraction of an intellect formulating all its evidence and carefully estimating the probability thereof by a vulgar fraction by the size of whose denominator and numerator alone it is swayed, is ideally as inept as it is actually impossible. It is almost incredible that men who are themselves working philosophers should pretend that any philosophy can be, or ever has been, constructed without the help of personal preference, belief, or divination. How have they succeeded in so stultifying their sense for the living facts of human nature as not to perceive that every philosopher, *or man of science either* [my emphasis], whose initiative counts for anything in the evolution of thought, has taken his stand on a sort of dumb conviction that the truth must lie in one direction rather than another, and a sort of preliminary assurance that his notion can be made to work; and has borne his best fruit in trying to make it work?

[9] Gerald E. Myers, *William James: His Life and Thought* (New Haven, 1986), p. 564.

These mental instincts in different men are the spontaneous variations upon which the intellectual struggle for existence is based. The fittest conceptions survive, and with them the names of their champions shining to all futurity.[10]

James's Methodological Monism

In the above passage James goes beyond saying that *in fact* intellect, will, taste, and passion operate together in the formation of all beliefs, whether philosophical, religious, or scientific, for he holds that it would be "ideally inept" to think that there is *any* belief that is not established in this complex way. I emphasize this because at least one commentator has portrayed James as if he thought that different kinds of statements are supported in fundamentally different ways: those of empirical science by discovering facts, those of pure mathematics and logic by seeing relations between ideas, and those which are metaphysical, moral, or esthetic by will, taste, and passion. When James said we accept or "trow" only those beliefs that work, A. J. Ayer thinks he meant to add that a factual belief works if and only if it is corroborated by experience; a mathematical or logical belief works if and only if it expresses a relationship between ideas that is "perceptively obvious at a glance"; and a moral, metaphysical, or esthetic belief works if and only if it brings satisfaction to the person who holds it.[11] It would follow from Ayer's interpretation that only moral, metaphysical, and esthetic beliefs are at the mercy of the will, taste, and passion. Those of natural science, mathematics, and logic would be deaf to the claims of feeling and sensory experience, whereas those of ethics, esthetics, metaphysics, and theology would respond to a person's every heartbeat.

---

[10] William James, "The Sentiment of Rationality," in *The Will to Believe and Other Essays in Popular Philosophy* (New York, 1898), pp. 92–93.

[11] A. J. Ayer, *The Origins of Pragmatism: Studies in the Philosophy of Charles Sanders Peirce and William James* (London, 1968), pp. 201–12.

In my opinion, many passages of James support this interpretation but there are also many that do not, because James was not clear or consistent on the issues involved. Ayer puts his finger on only one strain in James's thought, a strain that brought him close to logical positivism and, ironically, to the views of Jonathan Edwards and Emerson. Edwards added a sixth sense to the ordinary five of Locke, insisted that the Protestant elect have a "sense of the heart" which allows them to see the glory of divine things, and roundly attacked those who were content with a more theoretical or more historical knowledge of divine excellency. And while Emerson departed in many ways from Edwards's philosophy and theology, he too relied on his heart more than on his head when it came to his religious, moral, esthetic, and metaphysical convictions. That was Emerson's main point when urging that Coleridgian Reason could see the glory of God in the face of Jesus, the existence of Platonic ideas, and the truth of moral propositions. For Edwards, the Protestant saint could be a simple, ignorant man and yet see truth more readily than the man of learning or the philosopher; for Emerson, the poet who saw the highest truths could be a farmer or a child; and according to James in the *Varieties* and in *The Will to Believe*, a saint or religious genius has the right to accept a metaphysics or a religion that satisfied him even when his logical intellect, as James put it, was not coerced.

It is ironic that James should fit so easily into an earlier American tradition of anti-intellectualism when one concentrates on the positivistic strain in his thought, since positivism is so scientific in orientation.[12] Nevertheless, there is a strong tendency among logical positivists to treat ontological, religious, and ethical questions as radically different from scientific questions; some, like Carnap, hold that metaphysical questions such as "Are there physical objects?" and "Are there universals?" are not settled as we settle questions such as "Are there bacteria?" or "Are there electrons?" The latter

----

[12] See my *Science and Sentiment in America: Philosophical Thought from Jonathan Edwards to John Dewey* (New York, 1972), chap. 8.

questions Carnap regarded as factual questions that should be answered by empirical investigation, whereas he thought that the more general ontological questions call for decisions about the convenience of a whole conceptual framework, decisions that he regarded as justified by appealing to pragmatic considerations. And although, as I have said, there are passages in James that justify viewing him in this way, especially one in *Pragmatism* where he tells us that "2 + 2 = 4" is tested in one way and "sensible truths" in another,[13] the long passage above in which he speaks of the roles of taste and passion in establishing *all* beliefs reveals a different strain in James's view of scientific "trowing," to use his archaism.

A related strain is evident at points in *Pragmatism* where James avoids the notion that we test our beliefs individually. There he sometimes leans toward the holistic view that when we suppose we are testing an isolated belief, whether metaphysical, scientific, or logical, we are implicitly evaluating what he called a "stock of opinions" that is variously composed and subject simultaneously to tests of logical consistency, experience, and emotion. This position comes out most clearly in the following passage:

> The individual has a stock of old opinions already, but he meets a new experience that puts them to a strain. Somebody contradicts them; or in a reflective moment he discovers that they contradict each other; or he hears of facts with which they are incompatible; or desires arise in him which they cease to satisfy. The result is an inward trouble to which his mind till then had been a stranger, and from which he seeks to escape by modifying his previous mass of opinions. He saves as much of it as he can, for in this matter of belief we are all extreme conservatives. So he tries to change first this opinion, and then that (for they resist change very variously), until at last some new idea comes up which he can graft upon the ancient stock with a minimum of disturbance of the latter, some idea that mediates between the stock

---

[13] William James, *Pragmatism*, [ed. Fredson Bowers and Ignas K. Skrupskelis] (Cambridge, Mass., 1975), pp. 100–101.

and the new experience and runs them into one another most felici-
tously and expediently. This new idea is then adopted as the true one.
It preserves the older stock of truths with a minimum of modification,
stretching them just enough to make them admit the novelty, but conceiving that in ways as familiar as the case leaves possible.[14]

Here James does not say that physics is tested in one way, logic in
a second, and metaphysics in a third. His point is rather that a whole
thinker subjects a heterogeneous stock of opinions to a test in which
logical consistency, and conformity to both experience *and* desire, is
to be taken into account—in other words, that a whole thinker balances considerations of intellect, will, taste, and passion in an effort
to deal with the challenge that has put the old stock to a strain. And
although James recognizes the need to preserve that stock with a
minimum of modification, he regards even the oldest truths in the
old stock—those of logic and mathematics—as modifiable in the face
of a challenge from the experience. "How plastic even the oldest
truths . . . really are," he announces, "has been vividly shown in our
day by the transformation of logical and mathematical ideas."[15] This,
I suggest, is the James who encourages us to reject sharp distinctions
between mathematics and natural science, between natural science
and morals, and between natural science and religion. This is the
James who looks forward, though not altogether clearly, to a holistic
epistemology that I discuss at greater length in a later chapter; and
it differs from the James who persisted in holding with Locke and
Hume that mathematical truths depend on the relations between
ideas. This is the James whom Russell regarded as a holist in 1909,
and the James whose methodological monism anticipated views that
Alfred Tarski and W. V. Quine advanced forty years later.

I want to repeat, however, that James approached religion with a
deep interest in epistemology. As a philosopher he argued that a

---

[14] Ibid., pp. 34–35. W. V. Quine's phrase "minimum mutilation" is in part an echo of
James's "minimum of modification."

[15] Ibid., p. 37.

saint's feeling is direct evidence for the saint's belief in God, held that the goodness of a belief and its truth are intimately connected, and also declared that a mystic might say with justice that the anti-mystic is blind. Though James was a supernaturalist, he tried to support his view by appealing to the emotional experiences of saints and to his own feeling that religious beliefs were good for life. So, whatever one thinks of the cogency of his views on religious belief, one must recognize that he encouraged a conception of philosophy that did not pare it down to the philosophy of natural science. Despite his inconsistency and unclarity at points, he espoused an early form of epistemological holism, anticipating later philosophical doctrines that rejected sharp distinctions between the analytic and the synthetic, and between the *a priori* and the *a posteriori*. He regarded the philosophy of religion as an empirical discipline and he pointed the way to a holistic pragmatism that applies to ethics, as we shall see more fully in later chapters, especially in chapter 10. There it will be evident that the view that a moral thinker tests a conjunction of descriptive and normative beliefs by seeing whether that conjunction organizes her sensory experiences *and* her moral feelings owes something to James's views on the role of feeling and, of course, to the school of British moralists who spoke of a moral sense.

III

John Dewey's Philosophy of Art

LIKE WILLIAM JAMES, HIS REVERED PREDECESSOR
in the history of pragmatism, John Dewey
thought that philosophy was much more than philosophy of natural science. He respected and valued science, he tried to describe its method, he used it in defending many of his beliefs, and he thought that using it in what he called political technology would help solve many of our social problems. But Dewey did not think science is the only part of culture that a philosopher could and should examine; like James, he cast his net more widely. He wrote on history, education, religion, art, and law; he was an active political liberal, an influential leader of educational reform, and a highly beneficial force in American society during the twentieth century. Much of his thinking on these and other matters was dominated by his antipathy to the rationalism and the mind-body dualism of Descartes; but like Hume and William James, Dewey did not fully escape from the influence of classical rationalism, and occasionally lapsed into the mind-body dualism that he elsewhere deplored. Such lapses are evident at some points in Dewey's philosophy of art, a part of the philosophy of culture to which he devoted his *Art as Experience*, and one in which he struck a blow for philosophical freedom by showing that the philosopher is not restricted to analyzing statements of science but may also describe the artist's activity in psychological terms.

Dewey on the Roots of Art and Its Relations with Science

Dewey characterized his reflections on art as empirical, but in his earliest days he had been an admirer of Hegel, whose idea that an objective mind or spirit is manifested in social or cultural institutions left what Dewey referred to as a permanent deposit in his own thinking. Hegel's metaphysical ideas, Dewey said, dropped out of his philosophy and were replaced by "the idea, upon an empirical basis, of the power exerted by cultural environment in shaping the ideas, beliefs, and intellectual attitudes of individuals." Hegel also encouraged Dewey to make use of the concepts of continuity and conflict, which Dewey tried to interpret empirically when he read Darwin; he came to speak less in terms of the Hegelian dialectic and more about the interaction of the organism and its environment.[1] Partly because of the influence of Hegel and Darwin, the ideas of genesis, evolution, and development loomed large in Dewey's thinking, as they did for several American thinkers of the early twentieth century—among them the economist Thorstein Veblen, the jurist Oliver Wendell Holmes, Jr., and the political scientist Charles Beard. All of them participated in what I have called a revolt against formalism in economics, law, and political thought that was fueled in part by their interest in historical analysis and what was then called genetic method.[2] Dewey tried to use this method in his philosophy of art. He emphasized that not only music but all artistic production and perception takes place in time, and he devoted particular attention to the continuity between art and more primitive forms of biological interaction between the organism and its environment; he also rejected the separation of artistic production from science and

[1] "Biography of John Dewey," ed. Jane M. Dewey, in *The Philosophy of John Dewey*, ed. Paul Arthur Schilpp (Evanston, Ill., 1939), pp. 17–18.

[2] See Morton White, *Social Thought in America: The Revolt against Formalism* (New York, 1949; paperback edition with new foreword, New York, 1976).

everyday life. In tracing the origins of art and science, he connected them with animal life below the human scale, saying in *Art as Experience* that "because experience is the fulfillment of an organism in its struggles and achievements in a world of things, it is art in germ."[3]

No creature, Dewey said, lives merely under its skin. Its subcutaneous organs are a means of connection with the environment to which it must adjust if it is to survive. Life, he pointed out, consists of phases in which the organism falls out of step with the environment and later recovers unison with it. In a vein reminiscent of Hegel's statements on dialectical development, Dewey asserted that such recovery is never a mere return to a prior state, since a growing life is enriched by the resistance through which it successfully passes. If the gap between organism and environment is too wide, the organism dies; if its activity is not enhanced by its encounter with its surroundings, it merely subsists. It will grow only when a temporary falling out with the environment is followed by what Dewey called a more extensive balance of the energies of the organism with those of the conditions under which it lives. Though Dewey thought the artist cares particularly for that phase of experience in which harmony is achieved, he maintained that the artist does not shun moments of resistance and tension but cultivates them because of their role in producing an immediately satisfying experience. By contrast, he said, the scientist is primarily interested in resolving tension between observation and thought, and unlike the artist, he uses his resolution of such tension as a stepping-stone to further inquiries.

Dewey went on to say something that typified his attempt to bridge what he often called dualistic separations. The difference between the esthetic and the intellectual, he said, is not sharp; it is a matter of "the places where emphasis falls in the constant rhythm that marks the interaction of the live creature with its surroundings" (p. 15). This idea of emphasis figured heavily in Dewey's effort to characterize the similarity between art and science, as in his observa-

---

[3] John Dewey, *Art as Experience* (New York, 1934), p. 19. This edition is hereafter cited parenthetically in the text.

tion that "The odd notion that an artist does not think and a scientific inquirer does nothing else is the result of converting a difference of tempo and emphasis into a difference of kind" (p. 15). Dewey held that the scientist's goal is a relatively remote one, reached by long trains of argument employing symbols and mathematical signs, whereas the painter's medium—colors and lines, for example—lies so close to the object produced that it merges into that object. For Dewey, however, this difference between art and science is one of degree but not of kind. He held that art develops and accentuates what is characteristically valuable in the enjoyments of everyday life and that the product of art issues from everyday experience as dyes come out of coal tar products when they receive special treatment (p. 11). He sought to understand the work of art, but not as an *a priori* theorist who arrived at his philosophical conclusions through the use of pure reason.

To understand the title of *Art as Experience*, we need to keep in mind Dewey's distinction between what he calls experience at large and *an* experience. Experience at large, he said, occurs continuously in the life of an individual, and it can be inchoate if we are distracted, interrupted, or lethargic. By contrast, we occasionally have what Dewey calls *an* experience. "That *was* an experience!" we sometimes exclaim after playing a good game of chess, eating a fine meal, or playing a tennis match. *An* experience is rounded out and closes with a consummation; it is a history, Dewey says, whose successive parts flow freely and seamlessly into what follows them. It has a single quality that pervades it in spite of the difference of its constituent parts, but its unity is not called emotional, practical, or intellectual until we think about it and find that it is predominantly of one type or another. An experience that is predominantly intellectual, he says, also has an esthetic quality and differs from a predominantly artistic experience only in its emphases and materials. Furthermore, Dewey says, a predominantly intellectual and a predominantly artistic experience may both have a satisfying emotional quality that is immediately felt when either is consummated. It should be noted, however,

that an immediately felt experience is different from an experience
of going through the process of creating a work of art and from
engaging in a scientific experiment. The difference is like that between the experience of joy that a victorious tennis player has at the
end of a match and the playing of the whole match that Dewey calls
"*an* experience," or like that between the immediate experience at
the conclusion of an experiment and the entire experiment.

Dewey emphasizes, however, that during the creative process the
artist, like the scientist, uses his intelligence to grasp the connection
between an action and its consequences: "A painter must consciously
undergo the effect of his every brush stroke or he will not be aware
of what he is doing and where his work is going . . .; he has to see
each particular connection of doing and undergoing in relation to
the whole he desires to produce" (p. 45). Dewey argues that philosophers who identify thinking with the use of the special material of
words fail to see that thinking effectively about relations of colors,
volumes, and lines, as a painter does, is just as demanding. Indeed,
he goes further and says that "since words are easily manipulated in
mechanical ways, the production of a work of genuine art probably
demands more intelligence than does most of the so-called thinking
that goes on among those who pride themselves on being 'intellec-
tuals' " (p. 46). An artist must have knowledge that is conveyed in
what Dewey, under the influence of Charles Peirce, regarded as a
statement which says what a person, whether artist or scientist, will
directly experience upon performing a certain operation. For
Dewey there is a difference between an experiment as a whole—
which Dewey calls *an* experience—and the perception that consum-
mates it—an *immediate* experience. Dewey expresses this distinction
in other terms by saying that during an ordinary experience, as well
as during an artistic or scientific experience, an individual (a) does
something, (b) has an immediate experience of enjoyment, and (c)
notes the causal connection between his doing and enjoying. Dewey
remarks, however, that the word "artistic" ordinarily refers to the
act of production (doing), whereas the word "esthetic" ordinarily

refers to the perception and enjoyment (undergoing); this usage, he thinks, encourages a mechanical separation of artistic production and esthetic perception when in fact they are organically related. In order to underscore the organic character of this relation between doing and enjoying, Dewey applies the hyphenated term "artistic-esthetic" to what a painter, poet, musician, composer, or architect does. But the fact that production and immediate perception are organically related does not make them identical; he says it links them in the way that members of an organism are linked rather than mechanically.

In addition to calling attention to the similarity between predominantly artistic experiences or productions and predominantly scientific experiences or experiments, and in addition to tracing them to their biological roots, Dewey presents a general description of the main features of *an* artistic-esthetic experience. To describe it, he says, is to describe the stages by which it moves toward its goal, stages he lists in order as cumulation, tension, conservation, anticipation, and consummation. Dewey begins his discussion of these stages with a remark about the everyday process through which an ordinary person goes when furnishing a room. The person, he says, tries to form an agreeable ensemble by seeing to it that tables, chairs, rugs, lamps, wall color, and spacing of fixtures do not clash since the person wishes to avoid confusion in perceiving the finished room. For if there is confusion, "vision cannot then complete itself" (p. 136). It will be broken up into a succession of disconnected seeings, but no mere succession is a series, according to Dewey. When, on the other hand, masses are balanced, colors harmonized, and lines and plane meet and intersect fittingly, perception of them is serial and grasps the whole because each sequential act of vision builds up and reinforces what went before. The artist's movement toward his goal begins with a period of cumulation in which the colors, lines, and planes of a painting begin to mass and cohere with each other until a period of tension emerges. Without the tension that arises when difficulties are encountered, there would be a mere explosive discharge of energy, an uncontrolled rush, and no development to-ward fulfillment. These difficulties require the use of intelligence by the artist, who is helped by a stock or fund of ideas that he calls upon. During the earlier phase of artistic production there is suspense and anticipation of resolution, and during the final consummatory phase there is always something new. "The unexpected turn, something which the artist himself does not definitely foresee, is a condition of the felicitous quality of a work of art; it saves it from being mechani-cal. . . . The painter and poet like the scientific inquirer know the delights of discovery" (p. 139).

Dewey's description of these stages might seem applicable only to the process of artistic production and not to esthetic perception or enjoyment, but Dewey insists that it applies equally to the latter. He not only makes the obvious point that an artist who is a producer must be an esthetic perceiver but he also says that an esthetic per-ceiver who is not an artist must be creative. In illustrating the first point, he says that when a person whittles, carves, sings, dances, molds, draws, or paints, his doing or making is artistic just in case the anticipated perceived qualities of his end-in-view or aim control or direct his doing or making. That is why the artist must appreciate and perceive while he works. Even if we think of art as an endeavor after perfection in execution, we must realize that such perfection cannot be defined in terms of execution alone and that we must refer to the reaction of a person who enjoys the work that is executed, whether or not that person is the artist. In developing his idea that artistic production and esthetic enjoyment are organically related, Dewey points out that until the artist arrives at a satisfying perception of what he is making, he continues shaping and reshaping; he moves his hand with an etching needle or brush while his eye constantly attends to and registers the consequences of what he does. However, the hand and the eyes "act as organs of the whole being," as they do not when there is merely a mechanical sequence of the seeing eye and the moving hand. When the experience is genuinely esthetic and organic, hand and eye are "instruments through which the entire live creature, moved and active throughout, operates" (p. 50).

In arguing his second point, that perception as well as production must be active, Dewey remarks that it is hard to see this when we think about perception only as it occurs in a person who does not produce art but who merely appreciates it. "We are given to supposing", Dewey says, that the perceiver who is not an artist "merely takes in what is there in finished form, instead of realizing that *this taking in involves activities that are comparable to those of the creator*" (p. 52; my emphasis). The receptivity of such a perceiver, Dewey maintains, is not to be confused with passivity since, like the creator's activity, the perceiver's reception of the work is a process consisting of a series of responsive acts that accumulate toward objective fulfillment. According to Dewey, when we do not go through this process, we do not perceive but merely recognize something; for him bare recognition is perception arrested before it has a chance to develop freely. In merely recognizing another person in a glancing way, we do not see him; but when we see him, "there is an act of reconstructive doing, and consciousness becomes fresh and alive. *This* act of seeing involves the cooperation of motor elements, as well as the cooperation of all funded ideas that may serve to complete the new picture that is forming." That is why a mere glance or glimpse "involves no stir of the organism, no inner commotion", whereas "an act of perception proceeds by waves that extend serially throughout the entire organism. There is, therefore, no such thing in perception as seeing or hearing *plus* emotion. The perceived object or scene is emotionally pervaded throughout" (p. 53).

When Dewey says that the receptivity of the perceiver of art is not passivity, he means that esthetic "perception is an act of the going-out of energy in order to receive, not a withholding of energy" (p. 53). We must summon our energy and pitch it at a responsive key in order to *take in* the object. To perceive, therefore, "a beholder must *create* his own experience. And his creation must include rela-

tions comparable to those which the original producer underwent."
These relations are not literally the same, he adds, but the perceiver,
like the artist, must order the elements of a whole in a process that
is similar in form to the process of organization that the creator of
the work consciously goes through. "Without an act of recreation
[by the beholder] the object is not perceived as a work of art. The
artist selected, simplified, clarified, abridged and condensed according to his interest. The beholder must go through these operations according to his point of view and interest. . . . There is work
done on the part of the percipient as there is on the part of the artist"
(p. 54). In assimilating esthetic appreciation and artistic creation in
this way, Dewey sought to eliminate yet another separation that he
thought traditional philosophy encouraged.

Dewey on Criticism

After arguing that the ordinary perceiver of art is active and creative,
Dewey goes on to characterize criticism similarly, but his route to
this characterization is sometimes confusing and, it seems to me,
inconsistent. Dewey denies that the primary task of the critic is to
evaluate a work as good or bad and he also denies that the critic's
job is limited to what Dewey calls "a direct ejaculation" about the
work. However, when the critic has a direct reaction, his criticism,
Dewey declares at one point, is a search for the properties of the
object that may justify that reaction (p. 308). Presenting these properties is the main task of the critic, he says; but when he also says
that calling attention to them may *justify* the critic's reaction, Dewey
may be fairly asked what justification amounts to. More particularly,
he may be asked whether there are any general principles that serve
as logical bridges from the properties discerned by the critic to his
direct and justified reaction. That Dewey would deny the existence
of such principles is clear from the sharp attack he mounts on what
he calls judicial criticism. He argues that such criticism appeals to

eternal principles that cannot cope with the emergence of new modes of life or with experiences that demand new modes of artistic expression. Judicial criticism, he thinks, tends to be legalistic and formalistic; it worships old masters and techniques that are often outdated. Its defects, he says, provoke a reaction to the opposite extreme that he calls impressionistic criticism, because it "reacts from the standardized 'objectivity' of ready-made rules and precedents to the chaos of a subjectivity that lacks objective control" (p. 304). Because judicial criticism sets up false notions of objective values and objective standards, impressionist critics deny there are objective values at all (p. 306). And in opposition to impressionist critics, Dewey insists that there are objective values—but on this subject his views are not very clear.

Dewey maintains that the critic who operates objectively does not employ an officially determined standard like that establishing the meter. Such a critic judges but he does not measure a work of art as one would measure the length of a log by comparing it with a bar deposited in Paris or anywhere else, since there is no external and public thing, defined by law to be the same for all transactions, that can be physically applied by the critic (p. 307). However, Dewey says, "it does not follow because of the absence of an uniform and publicly determined external object, that objective criticism of art is impossible". Yet when Dewey tells us here what he thinks objective criticism is, he seems to forget that he has said earlier that the critic presents descriptive properties that may *justify* the critic's direct reaction to the object. While seeming to forget this, Dewey says that if the critic's search is sincere and informed, "it is not, when it is undertaken, concerned with values but with the objective properties of the object under consideration" (p. 308). Here, the critic's concern *to justify* his ejaculation or his evaluation seems to disappear, replaced by a concern with merely describing a painting's colors, lights, and volumes in their relations to one another. In this moment of forgetfulness, Dewey declares, the critic should report the objective traits of a work without focusing "upon values in the sense of excellent and poor." Dewey now says that the critic's purely descriptive judgments may help "in the direct experience of others, as a survey of the country is helpful to one who travels through it, while dicta about worth operate to limit personal experience" (p. 309). When the Deweyan critic refrains from issuing dicta about worth, he resembles a noncommittal observer who describes an action as a lie but who refrains from saying whether it ought to be performed. Other moralists, in contrast, present moral principles such as the Ten Commandments as bridges between the described properties of the action and its being one that ought or ought not to be performed. But unlike these other moralists, a critic of art, according to Dewey, should not present esthetic principles or make singular judgments of worth because of Dewey's distrust of judicial criticism and his avoidance of what he calls limiting dicta about worth.

Dewey's lack of interest in esthetic principles that are analogous to moral principles suggests that he may think that a critic who likes a work can say only that he likes it because it has certain descriptive properties while admitting that others may not be caused to like it. In other words, the critic makes a causal statement that links his liking with certain objective properties. Consequently we can imagine someone addressing a Deweyan critic as follows: "I agree that the work has the properties you have mentioned, and I grant that they caused your favorable reaction to the work. But those properties of the work do not cause *me* to have a favorable reaction to it. After all, Professor Dewey allows that since you and I are different organisms with different characteristics, my interaction with the work may not lead me to respond to it as you do." Presumably the Deweyan critic cannot say that his interlocutor *ought* to like the work, because in *Art as Experience* Dewey does not hold a view like the one he had adopted in *The Quest for Certainty* (1929) concerning desirability or what ought to be desired. In the latter work he holds that a thing may be desired but not desirable, whereas in *Art as Experience* Dewey does not say that a work of art may be liked and yet not be worthy of being liked. At points Dewey seems averse to saying that a work of art ought to be liked because of his aversion to judicial criticism and his avoidance of "dictations of what the attitude of any one should be" in esthetic matters (p. 309), and at such points Dewey seems to advocate a relativism in esthetic criticism that he does not advocate in ethics. In ethics he says that we have an obligation or right to desire something if and only if a normal person would, whereas in esthetics he does not say that we have an obligation or right to like a work of art if and only if a certain kind of viewer would. For Dewey the critic merely calls attention to descriptive properties of the painting and does no more for the ordinary viewer than what a mapmaker does for the tourist.

At other points, however, Dewey makes a distinction among objective properties of the work, some of which he calls "valued properties" that are not mere ejaculations. Though generally wary about using the word "beauty", he says that it is "a short term for certain valued qualities" (p. 251) of a work of art and that beauty should not be regarded as something in the mind which is projected into the work. He argues that this view is based on the faulty view that beauty is first in the mind and then projected into the painting whereas the painting's other properties are "out there" and not projected. Against this, Dewey argues that the interaction between the landscape which is not objectively yellow and its being seen as yellow by a person with jaundice does not differ fundamentally from the interaction between a landscape which *is* objectively yellow and its being seen as yellow by a person with normal vision. Dewey holds that *all* the perceived properties of the painting—its valued properties and its other properties—are the results of interactions between microscopic entities and the perceiving of an organism. Those microscopic entities are identified by Dewey as vibrations of light from pigments on canvas that are reflected and refracted; he also says that they are the atoms, electrons, and protons studied by physicists and that *all* the perceived properties of the picture are produced by the interaction of these physical entities with what the mind through the organism contributes.

From this it follows, according to Dewey, that the beauty of the picture perceived when physical particles and the organism interact "belongs to the picture just as much as do the rest of its properties" (p. 251). The beauty or valued property is no more "in us" than the rest of the picture's properties are, and so the picture's beauty is on a par with every other property of the picture. Dewey holds that the physicist's atoms, electrons, and protons may interact with one organism or individual so as to lead that organism to attribute one color to the painting, whereas they may interact with another organism so as to lead that other organism to attribute a different color to the painting. Thus, if a person of normal vision says that an abstract painting of a rectangle is white, another person who has jaundice may say that the painting is yellow. Dewey says the same thing about the attribution of beauty; therefore the critic may truthfully say "Beautiful" whereas the ordinary person says "Not beautiful" when they both look at the same picture. In that case, according to Dewey, the critic has no privileged position and should not be regarded as a judge whose attribution of beauty is preferable to or favored over a different attribution by an ordinary person. Here Dewey says that we may attribute the property of beauty to a painting instead of merely saying that we like it, but he does not regard the professional critic's attribution of beauty as authoritative by comparison to the ordinary viewer's attribution of it.

However, Dewey also says that the critic is as creative as an artist, and with that statement his view of the critic's standing seems to change. Dewey now says that "the material out of which [the critic's] judgment grows is the work, the object, but it is this object as it enters into the experience of the critic by interaction with his own sensitivity and his knowledge and funded store from past experiences." For this reason, the properties the critic attributes to the work vary "with the concrete material that evokes them and that must sustain them if criticism is pertinent and valid" (pp. 309–10). Such variation permits the critic to be creative, as we can see in

Dewey's characterization of the two functions that critical judgments perform, analysis or discrimination, and synthesis or unification—especially synthesis. Analysis, he says, evokes a clearer consciousness of the constituent parts of the object, whereas synthesis shows how these parts form a whole. Since "one and the same work of art presents different designs and different facets to different observers—as a sculptor may see different figures in a block of stone"—one mode of synthesis "on the part of the critic is as legitimate as another." But Dewey then adds a crucial proviso. He says not only that the design must be "really present in the work" but, more important, that it must be "significant" (p. 314). However, he also insists that "no rules can be laid for the performance of so delicate an act as determination of the significant parts of the whole, and of their respective places and weights in the whole"; therefore "criticism becomes itself an art" (pp. 310, 313). After giving the impression that the critic's reaction to a painting is no better than anyone else's, Dewey now allows that a good critic has some kind of authority: the good critic sees *significant design* where the bad critic presumably does not.

Moreover, Dewey singles out the characteristics that an authoritative critic must have just as he singles out the characteristic that an ideal moral critic must have. The authoritative critic must have "a consuming informed interest" in the work of art, for "without natural sensitivity connected with an intense liking for certain subject-matters, a critic, having even a wide range of learning, will be so cold that there is no chance of his penetrating the heart of a work of art. He will remain on the outside." Dewey immediately adds that "unless affection is informed with insight that is the product of a rich and full experience, judgment will be one-sided or not rise above the level of gushy sentimentalism" (p. 310). To attain this informed insight, Dewey says, the authoritative critic must be familiar with the various traditions of the work he judges, be intimately acquainted with many works in those traditions, and be familiar with the development of the artist whose work he is criticizing. In that case the good critic *is* distinguished from others and to that extent has privileged access to the esthetic merit of the work that an ordinary perceiver or a bad critic lacks. In my opinion, therefore, Dewey oscillates between a relativism that puts the critic on the same level as any ordinary judge of a work and a doctrine that makes a good critic authoritative because he discerns the *significant* features of a work even though he has no rules for determining significance. Such a critic is very different from one who surveys a work as a cartographer surveys a country and who offers no dicta of worth to the traveler. In this respect the art critic plays a role that is comparable to that of the informed moral critic in Dewey's ethical theory.

Dewey against Dualism

We have seen that Dewey contrasts having an experience with what he calls a direct or immediate experience; but when he says that his direct experience is *caused* by an interaction between an organism and the environment, he may be asked whether he identifies a direct experience independently of its being caused by that interaction. If he says that he observes introspectively that he is having a direct experience *caused* by the interaction, he would seem to accept a dichotomy or dualism between his inside direct experience and the external interaction that causes it. But if he says that the statement "Dewey is now having a direct experience of joy" is not causally but analytically related to a statement describing an interaction between him and the environment, he seems to accept a dualism between the analytic and the synthetic that he severely criticizes in some of his writings. For it would seem that if he denies that the relation is causal, he might be tempted to say that it is what he calls ideational, which is close to saying that it is analytic.

Dewey's ambiguity on this issue is evident in what he says about the status of logical and mathematical truth on the one hand and truth in natural science on the other. Since I have discussed Dewey's views on this subject elsewhere,[4] I shall be as brief as possible here. In the 1920s, Dewey tried to avoid rationalistic dualism by calling logic an empirical discipline that gives an organized and tested descriptive account of the way in which thought actually goes on.[5] He also said in the 1920s that although "mathematics is often cited as an example of purely normative thinking dependent upon *a priori* canons and supra-empirical material . . ., it is hard to see how the student who approaches the matter historically can avoid the conclusion that the status of mathematics is as empirical as that of metallurgy."[6] In 1929 Dewey declared that a sharp Humeian distinction between truths about relations of ideas and truths about matters of fact was a remnant of the unacceptable classical dualism according to which philosophy employs "a method issuing from reason itself, and having the warrant of reason, independently of experience."[7] In parts of his *Logic*, which appeared in 1938, Dewey continued to avoid an epistemological dualism between logic and natural science by saying that what Peirce called logical leading principles differ from the leading principles of physics only in the width of their application. But, for reasons I do not fully understand, Dewey came to adopt a different view in other parts of the same work when he distinguished between "existential propositions," which refer directly to actual conditions as determined by experimental observation, and "ideational or conceptual" propositions, which are applicable to existence through the operations they represent as possibilities.[8] One might think Dewey would have regarded this sharp distinction as objectionable, yet he uses it in order to support

[4] See "Experiment and Necessity in Dewey's Philosophy" in my *Pragmatism and the American Mind: Essays and Reviews in Philosophy and Intellectual History* (New York, 1973), pp. 138–54; see also my *Science and Sentiment in America: Philosophical Thought from Jonathan Edwards to John Dewey* (New York, 1972), chap. 11.

[5] John Dewey, *Philosophy and Civilization* (New York, 1931), p. 129.

[6] John Dewey, *Reconstruction in Philosophy* (New York, 1920), p. 135.

[7] John Dewey, *The Quest for Certainty: A Study of the Relation of Knowledge and Action* (New York, 1929), p. 27.

[8] John Dewey, *Logic: The Theory of Inquiry* (New York, 1938), pp. 146–47, 283–84.

a distinction between two kinds of propositions that others have
called synthetic and analytic. It seems, therefore, that Dewey has no
consistent view to which he can appeal when asked how he links
a statement about direct experience and one about an interaction
between the organism and the environment.

At places Dewey tries to avoid mind-body dualism by saying that
the self and its direct experience are absorbed in the interaction between organism and environment as hydrogen and oxygen are absorbed in water when they combine (*Art as Experience*, p. 250), and
Dewey's disciple Sidney Hook tells us on his behalf that an esthetic
experience is not *in* the environment nor in the subject, but "in the
interacting relation of the two."[9] But what does this amount to? If
the statement that connects the relation of interaction with the experience is "ideational," Dewey is involved in the dualism between
the analytic and the synthetic. But if the interaction *produces* the
experience, Dewey will once again be involved in the dualism between the outside interaction and the inside direct experience. We
therefore find Dewey in a dilemma; he is caught between mind-
body dualism and the dualism of the analytic and the synthetic.

Dewey against Reductive Criticism

I want now to consider a related problem that faces Dewey when he
criticizes theories of art associated with the names of Marx and
Freud. Dewey criticizes some of their followers for committing what
he calls the fallacy of reduction. This fallacy is committed, he says,
"when some constituent of the work of art is isolated and then the
whole is reduced to terms of this single isolated element" (p. 315).
In other words, Dewey objects to criticism that "reduces" pictures
like Titian's to economic documents on the basis of his depiction of
aristocracy and commercial wealth that is "incidentally inside them"
(pp. 315–16). Dewey also puts much of psychoanalytic criticism into

---

[9] Sidney Hook, *John Dewey: An Intellectual Portrait* (New York, 1939), p. 202.

this category because it treats factors that may or may not have "played a part in the causative generation of a work of art as if they 'explained' the esthetic content of the work of art itself." Dewey argues against what he calls reductionism by saying that the work "is just what it is whether a father or a mother fixation, or a special regard for the susceptibilities of a wife, entered into its production." He also remarks that "historical and cultural information may throw light on the causes" of the production of literary works, "but when all is said and done, each one is just what it is artistically, and its esthetic merits are within the work. Knowledge of social conditions of production is, when it is really knowledge, of genuine value. But it is no substitute for understanding of the object in its own qualities and relations" (p. 316).

Here Dewey makes a sharp distinction between what his follower Hook calls the "immanent qualities" of a work[10] and those that are not immanent, and accuses so-called reductionists of confusing these two kinds of qualities. Dewey says that the work of art is what it is artistically and that Marxist and Freudian reductionists present properties of it that are at best causally rather than logically connected with what it is; but how does Dewey distinguish between properties that are immanent or logically inherent in a work and those that are not? How can he make a distinction between properties that are essential to a work of art and those that are not essential to it when he inveighs against theorists of art and literary critics who are, as he says, in thrall to the ancient metaphysics of essence (p. 216)? How can Dewey say that the work of art is "just what it is whether a father or mother fixation, or a special regard for the susceptibilities of a wife, entered into its production" without accepting something like a distinction between the essence of a work—what it is—and its accidents?

Dewey would not have had to face this question if he had said merely that the reductive fallacy "flourishes wherever some alleged occasion in the life of the artist, some biographical incident, is taken

---

[10] Ibid., p. 205.

as if it were a kind of substitute for *appreciation* of the poem that resulted" (p. 316; my emphasis). For then Dewey might say that *knowledge* of a biographical kind is different from, and therefore not a substitute for, *esthetic appreciation* of a poem—that is, direct enjoyment of it. But, as we have seen, Dewey holds in places that all the properties of a painting are on a par. So in what sense are some of these properties immanent but others not? Some properties of a work, according to Dewey, are fundamentally different from its property of having been created by someone with a "father or a mother fixation," but how can he distinguish between the property of being a picture in which a woman wears a blue dress and the property of being painted by someone fixated on blue dresses? If Dewey says that the blueness is immanent and the other property not, how does he make such a distinction without accepting a view that may put him in thrall to the ancient metaphysics of essence? Once again he seems to be caught in a dilemma that is related to more fundamental problems in his philosophy.

In my view, therefore, Dewey's contribution to the philosophy of art lies primarily in his recognition of the continuity between art and more primitive forms of interaction between the organism and its environment, in his recognition of the similarities between art and science, in his view of the stages of artistic creation, and in his view that the philosopher engages in empirical inquiry when defending these views. By contrast, when he characterizes the relations between what he calls direct experience and the interaction between the organism and the environment, when he distinguishes in his *Logic* between existential and ideational generalizations, and when he tries to distinguish between different kinds of properties that a work of art may have, he seems to be involved in dualisms that he deplores and thus in inconsistency.

In raising questions about some of Dewey's distinctions, I do not mean to disparage his attempt to present a naturalistic philosophy of art and esthetic criticism. He deserves great credit for making that attempt, for showing that philosophy of art is epistemically coordinate with philosophy of science, and for rejecting the idea that philosophy of science is philosophy enough. When he described the stages of the creative process, he opened the door to empirical philosophizing about other elements of culture such as education, law, politics, and history, much as James did when he described the varieties of religious experience. With this in mind I turn now to consider later efforts in the twentieth century to create a philosophy of culture that goes beyond James and Dewey in abandoning rationalism totally and in adopting a holistic pragmatism that was vaguely adumbrated by James and Dewey but never fully developed by them.

IV

The Dualisms of Earlier Pragmatism

Y AIM IN CALLING ATTENTION TO DEWEY'S lapses into rationalism was to show that one of rationalism's most vehement critics may well have succumbed to it. For if one thinks of pragmatism as the doctrine originated by Charles Peirce, advocated by James, applied by Dewey, and adopted to some extent by C. I. Lewis and W. V. Quine, one may safely say that Dewey alone held that all beliefs, including ethical ones, may be tested by appealing to the normal five senses. Yet Dewey not only succumbed to rationalism in his philosophy of science but, as we shall see, tried unsuccessfully to show that statements of moral obligation may be analyzed in accordance with Peirce's pragmatic theory of scientific meaning. Peirce's so-called scholastic realism appears to be incompatible with that theory of meaning, as James's theism certainly is; Lewis explicitly denied that statements of moral obligation can be tested empirically, and so did Quine. In this chapter I briefly survey the methodological pluralism espoused by most of these philosophers and in a later chapter call attention to some early efforts in the direction of a holistic pragmatism in Duhem and, surprisingly, in Russell—a pragmatism that I think should culminate in a methodological monism that applies to logic, physics, ethics, and esthetics.

I begin by considering Peirce's pragmatism and the view of scientific law that he espoused when he lowered his pragmatic guard.[1]

---

[1] The theme of this discussion was first developed in "Pragmatism and the Scope of Science," which appears in my *Pragmatism and the American Mind: Essays and Reviews in Philosophy and Intellectual History* (New York, 1973), pp. 95–109.

According to Peirce, statements containing laboratory words such as "hard," "heavy," and "lithium" may be translated into what he called statements of practice. He said that although every laboratory statement is logically equivalent to what he called a myriad of other statements, one type of equivalent is of special importance to the scientist, namely, that which states what sensory experiences an experimenter would have if he were to perform certain operations on an object like a diamond that is said to be hard. Peirce maintained that if a statement cannot be translated into such a pragmatic equivalent, it lacks scientific meaning, and that two statements mean the same thing if their pragmatic equivalents are the same.

One purpose of such translation, according to Peirce, was to eliminate what he called ontological metaphysics as pragmatically meaningless; but, ironically, he seemed to have run afoul of his own pragmatism when analyzing the concept of scientific law. He held that a statement like "The Hope Diamond is hard" is pragmatically equivalent to the statement "If the Hope Diamond is rubbed by anything else, a scratch will not appear on the diamond," and this equivalent of "The Hope Diamond is hard" may also be expressed by the law "Whenever another object rubs against the Hope Diamond, no scratch will appear on the diamond." But Peirce, as Arthur Burks has pointed out,[2] distinguished such a law from the universal statement "All of the books on my desk now are in English." He said these two universal statements are different because the law would entitle us to say "If a wooden toothpick, which had previously burned up, had rubbed against the Hope Diamond, no scratch would have appeared on the diamond," whereas the other universal statement—the nonlaw—would not entitle us to assert "If Gutenberg's first Bible were on my desk, it would be in English." In other words, a law supports a singular subjunctive conditional statement whereas a nonlaw does not. According to Peirce, some philosophers, whom he called nominalists, fail to make this distinction and main-

_____

[2] See Arthur W. Burks's introduction to the selection from the writings of C. S. Peirce in *Classic American Philosophers: Peirce, James, Royce, Santayana, Dewey, Whitehead: Selections from Their Writings*, ed. Max H. Fisch (New York, 1951), esp. p. 52.

tain that the law "Whenever another object rubs against the Hope Diamond, no scratch appears on the diamond" is equivalent to the statement "On all actual occasions on which another object rubs against the Hope Diamond, no scratch appears on the diamond." Nominalists, Peirce argued, say that a law is a generalization which asserts that on all *actual* occasions—past, present, or future—on which another object rubs against the Hope Diamond, no scratch appears on the diamond. Therefore, Peirce said, the nominalist thinks that laws refer only to "actualities" in the past, present, and future, whereas he, a realist, held that a law additionally says something about what he called "would-bes" that are expressed in subjunctive conditionals like the one about a destroyed toothpick.

Burks argued against Peirce that from a pragmatic point of view, there is no difference between Pierce's so-called scholastic realism and what Peirce called nominalism. According to Burks, an experimental scientist has no interest in saying that the rubbing of a destroyed toothpick would not have left a scratch if rubbed against the Hope Diamond, no interest in Peirce's would-bes. The truth of such a subjunctive conditional, Burks asserted, is beyond the experimenters' interest, for whatever they want to say may be said in the indicative mood. For this reason, Burks argued, Peirce's view of scientific law ran afoul of Peirce's own pragmatic maxim that a difference that makes no experimental difference may be disregarded. There is no pragmatic difference, Burks said, between nominalism and Peirce's view of law, because the latter adds nothing to the former that is of interest to the experimental scientist. Therefore Peirce's own pragmatism seems to undermine what he called his scholastic realism or his belief in the reality of *would-bes*.

Peirce's predicament was similar in some respects to that of William James in discussing the method of theology. By this I mean that if James had adopted Peirce's criterion of scientific meaning, which predicts what *sensory* experiences an experimenter will have, James would have had as much difficulty in squaring it with his acceptance of the belief that God exists as Peirce had in squaring his pragmatism with his realistic metaphysics. In *The Varieties of Religious Experience*, as we have seen, James supported his theism in two ways. One of them was to say that the feelings of the saint or mystic constituted empirical evidence for the religious hypothesis, a claim that required James to expand the notion of empirical evidence to include mystical feelings in addition to the familiar five sorts of experiences, and thereby to introduce a kind of experience that is not mentioned in Peirce's pragmatic theory of meaning. Furthermore, when James said in *Pragmatism* that believing in God *caused* him to have certain feelings that justified his belief in God, he departed in another way from Peirce's pragmatism. The latter was a theory of *the meaning* of a statement like "This diamond is hard" that translated it into one logically equivalent to it; but when James said that believing in God *causes* certain feelings, he was not speaking of the meaning or logical content of the belief. Instead, James was concerned with *the effect* of believing that God exists. Discovering meaning, in James's view, required an examination of the impact of the belief on the believer, not a logical examination of what "God exists" means. Small wonder, then, that Peirce once spoke scornfully of the man who said, "Oh, I could not believe so-and-so, because I should be wretched if I did."[3] James's accepting a strength-giving religious belief as true even though it was meaningless by Peirce's pragmatic standards was not unlike Peirce's accepting his realistic view of law as true even though the latter was meaningless by those same pragmatic standards. In short, neither Peirce nor James was fully consistent or thoroughgoing in the application of Peirce's pragmatic maxim. Peirce failed to apply it to his own realistic metaphysics, and James failed to follow its full implications in his discussion of theological belief.

Whereas Peirce abandoned a strict pragmatism when he defended a metaphysics of scholastic realism and James abandoned it when he accepted religious beliefs because they had strength-giving causal consequences, the ambivalence of the pragmatic movement was ob-

---

[3] Charles Sanders Peirce, *Collected Papers of Charles Sanders Peirce*, vol. 5, *Pragmatism and Pragmaticism*, ed. Charles Harshorne and Paul Weiss (Cambridge, Mass., 1960), para. 377.

vious in the field of ethics as well. John Dewey was an ethical naturalist who believed that all ethical statements are translatable into empirical statements, but C. I. Lewis, the most distinguished follower of Peirce in the generation after Dewey, emphatically disagreed. In the ethical writings of Lewis one finds an explicit acceptance of the view that some ethical knowledge is not based on empirical investigation, since he argued that knowledge of what is right and just is not determined by empirical facts alone. In other words, Dewey and Lewis were united in regarding statements of *value* as empirical, but they divided on the subject of obligation, of what ought to be done. On the subject of value, Dewey's view was close to that of Lewis, who says: "As a first approximation, we might say that attributing value to an existent, O, means that under circumstances C, O will or would lead to satisfaction in the experience of somebody, S; or it intends the joint assertion of many such affirmations."[4] Both Dewey and Lewis follow Peirce's pragmatic maxim by applying its central idea to statements of value; Lewis, like Dewey, says that value is a disposition and that attributing value to a diamond is like attributing hardness to it. In both cases, he argued, certain direct experiences will or would occur under certain circumstances, and in both cases we express scientific knowledge.

However, Lewis made a sharp distinction between value and obligation that upsets any picture of pragmatic uniformity on the fundamentals of ethics. In his own words, "Valuation is always a matter of empirical knowledge. But what is right and just, can never be determined by empirical facts alone."[5] By contrast, Dewey was not prepared to grant that there is a class of moral statements about obligations established by means that are fundamentally different

---

[4] Clarence Irving Lewis, *An Analysis of Knowledge and Valuation* (La Salle, Ill., 1946), p. 512.

[5] Ibid., p. 554. See also my "Value and Obligation in Dewey and Lewis," in *Pragmatism and the American Mind*, pp. 155–67; "Desire and Desirability: A Rejoinder to a Posthumous Reply by John Dewey," *Journal of Philosophy* 93 (1996): 229–42; and "Peirce's *Summum Bonum* and the Ethical Views of C. I. Lewis and John Dewey," *Philosophy and Phenomenological Research* 59 (1999): 1029–37.

from those used in science, but his efforts at defending his theory of obligation are not in my opinion persuasive. He maintained that the statement that an object ought to be desired means the same as the statement that a normal person would desire it leads to the view that the second purely descriptive statement means the same as a moral "ought"-statement, which seems hard to accept. Unlike Dewey, Lewis maintains that statements of moral obligation are different from those of empirical science, but he fails to make clear how we justify judgments of right and wrong if not by experience. His difficulty is related to his position on the nature of *a priori* knowledge, itself a subject on which pragmatists are in disagreement.

Lewis's theory of *a priori* knowledge, knowledge that we supposedly justify without reference to experience, was one of the more distinctive features of his work in epistemology. As we have seen, a traditional characteristic of such knowledge is its necessity—statements expressing such knowledge must be true; in contrast, *a posteriori* knowledge is said to be contingent—statements expressing it can be false. If *a posteriori* statements are true, that is not because they *must* be true but because the world happens to be as they say it is. According to Hume, *a priori* statements are made in pure mathematics whereas the most highly developed variety of *a posteriori* knowledge is to be found in the empirical sciences. The problem of *a priori* knowledge has often been conceived as the problem of saying how there could be such a thing, and a number of answers have been offered in the history of philosophy. The answer given by Lewis was one of the most widely accepted in the twentieth century and was in broad outline similar to that given by logical positivists. He held that all and only *a priori* statements are analytic: they may be seen to be true merely by inspecting the meanings of their component terms. Therefore he rejects Kant's doctrine of the synthetic *a priori*. In Lewis's view, the statement that every horse is an animal is true because the meaning of the word "horse" contains the meaning of the word "animal," and therefore we can discover its truth without observing horses. Consequently, analytic statements are sharply distinguished by Lewis from synthetic statements, whose truth we cannot determine merely by studying meanings. Like the logical positivists, Lewis held that all logical and mathematical truths are fundamentally like the statement that every horse is an animal, in that they are analytic. The upshot of Lewis's epistemology was an exhaustive and exclusive division of knowledge into that which requires no observation of the world for its justification and that which does, and so Lewis was involved in a serious problem over the status of statements about what is right and just. He contrasts them with value statements because he claims that value statements are empirical, but he cannot seriously hold that *all* statements about the rightness or wrongness of actions are analytic, seen to be true merely by an inspection of the meaning of their component terms. And since he rejects the positivistic view that ethical statements express no knowledge at all, he entered a quandary from which he never successfully emerged.

This brief discussion of *a priori* knowledge leads naturally to the question of pragmatism's position on the nature of mathematical and logical truth, and once again there is no position that is held by all pragmatists; indeed Peirce himself holds different views about it. One discerning expositor of Peirce's philosophy writes:

Peirce's Pragmatism is, primarily, the logic of hypothesis; its aim is to prescribe and articulate the one essential condition to which every genuine hypothesis must conform; and broadly this condition is that a hypothesis must be verifiable experimentally. This being the case, it would be natural to assume that Pragmatism has a bearing solely on questions of matters of fact, questions about the world which is disclosed to us, ultimately through our sensations. It should therefore have no bearing whatsoever on our purely formal *a priori* knowledge, that is, our knowledge of logical truths and of pure mathematics. But, although Peirce's writings on this issue are distressingly scrappy, there can be no doubt that he did *not* wish the scope of his Pragmatism to be restricted to thoughts, statements, or hypotheses concerning questions of empirical fact. Pragmatism, he maintains, has an important relevance to those parts of our knowledge which are commonly described as purely formal, or apodeictic.[6]

But while Peirce's writing on this subject may be "scrappy," Peirce's attempt to extend his pragmatism to the statements of logic and mathematics prefigures later pragmatic efforts to erase the sharp line between the analytic and the synthetic. Moreover, there is evidence that James too had serious doubts about the distinction between them, especially in the final chapter of his *Psychology*. It is titled "Necessary Truths and the Effects of Experience," and in one of its notes James says: "Some readers may expect me to plunge into the old debate as to whether the *a priori* truths are 'analytic' or 'synthetic.' It seems to me that the distinction is one of Kant's most unhappy legacies, for the reason that it is impossible to make it sharp."[7] Reflection on the sharpness of the distinction between analytic and synthetic statements led to a serious difference between pragmatists on the subject of logico-mathematical truth. Lewis espoused just such a sharp distinction as James both disowned in his *Psychology* and retained in that work and elsewhere.

On the other hand, W. V. Quine argued that his own refusal to make a sharp distinction between analytic and synthetic statements is more thoroughly pragmatic in spirit than the dualism of Lewis. Quine's attack on the distinction between analytic and synthetic was prompted by a number of considerations. It was inspired by the view that the meanings appealed to by Lewis in his account of analytic statements are obscure entities which lack a criterion for their identity, and by the view that the word "synonymous" as applied to linguistic expressions is also obscure because it lacks a behavioristic criterion. These and other considerations led Quine to the holistic conclusion that we must surrender the notion that for each kind of statement there is a separate and distinct method of validation which

---

[6] W. B. Gallie, *Peirce and Pragmatism* (Harmondsworth, Middlesex, 1952), p. 161.
[7] William James, *The Principles of Psychology* (New York, 1890), 2:661 [n. 2].

is based on the alleged fact that different kinds of statements are true of entities in different realms. He advanced this view in opposition not only to a sharp methodological distinction between logico-mathematical truth and truth in the natural sciences, but also to the contrast between ontology and natural science. Quine contends that there is a basic similarity in the methods of justifying statements of mathematics, statements of physics, and statements that assert the existence of universals—he holds that they are all justified empirically and pragmatically.[8] He may therefore be called a methodological monist so far as mathematics, the empirical sciences, and ontology are concerned, but we have seen that even such a qualified methodological monism has not been typical in the history of American pragmatism. Half-consciously, as in the case of Peirce and James, or explicitly, as in the case of Lewis, pragmatists have tended to deny the view that *all* statements that express knowledge may be tested empirically; even Quine shies away from a naturalistic or empirical view of ethics, as we shall see later.

Furthermore, as I pointed out in the previous chapter, Dewey wavered in his treatment of the distinction between *a priori* and *a posteriori* knowledge. More than any thinker in modern times, Dewey viewed the history of Western philosophy as a fruitless quest for certainty, a misguided effort to discover a class of truths that would be stable, certain, and self-evident; and that is why the notion of *a priori* knowledge was always suspect in his philosophy. Yet, as I maintained in chapter 3, Dewey makes a sharp distinction between what he calls "existential" and "ideational" propositions that resembles the positivistic distinction between synthetic and analytic propositions, and he does so on the basis of something like Peirce's distinction between a nominalistic and a realistic view of scientific law. In his *Logic*, Dewey distinguishes between (a) what he calls existential propositions beginning with the word "all" such as "All men have died or will die," which he calls a "spatio-temporal proposi-

---

[8] See W. V. Quine, "Two Dogmas of Empiricism," in *From a Logical Point of View: Nine Logico-Philosophical Essays* (Cambridge, Mass., 1953), pp. 20–46.

tion," and (b) what he calls an ideational or a universal "all"-proposition, which is a universal conditional statement such as "If anything is human, then it is mortal." The existential proposition is said by Dewey to be inductive or matter-of-fact, whereas the ideational or universal proposition is "valid . . . by definition of a conception."[9] He adds that the contrary-to-fact conditional statements of science are universal and therefore valid by definition, and he tells us that mathematical statements are universal because they are abstract hypothetical propositions. In addition, he says that all physical laws state a relation of characters in mathematical equations, and before he finishes his *Logic* he seems to adopt a view that is not completely removed from rationalism.

We may therefore sum up the views of the pragmatists I have considered as follows. Peirce's scholastic realism seemed to exempt some statements of ontology from his pragmatic theory of meaning; James's defense of mysticism seemed to exempt the statements of theology from it; Lewis explicitly exempted ethical statements in which we assert that actions are right or wrong; and Dewey fell into a variety of dualism when he distinguished existential and ideational statements. Finally, although Quine was a pragmatist and an empiricist in his approach to mathematics, logic, physics, and ontology, his pragmatism and empiricism virtually disappeared when he dealt with ethics. In short, not one of these five American philosophers who accepted pragmatism or have been associated with it successfully defended the view that *all* statements that are commonly said to express knowledge may be justified by the techniques commonly associated with empirical science. With this in mind, I turn first to certain holistic views that try to bridge some of these dualisms. After doing so I present a view that I accept and that I defend in later chapters, one that avoids a sharp epistemic distinction not only between logic and natural science but also between ethics and natural science.

---

[9] John Dewey, *Logic: The Theory of Inquiry* (New York, 1938), p. 256.

V

Early Epistemological Holism and the

Dualisms of Logical Empiricism

PIERRE DUHEM WAS A PHYSICIST AND PHILOSO-
pher of science who is not as well known as
some of the philosophers I have discussed so far, but he prepared
the way for the abandonment of rationalism and the emergence of
methodological monism as a theory of knowledge. Although
Duhem did not include mathematics in the system tested by experience, his holism as applied to physics paved the way for others who
extended it to beliefs in logic, in metaphysics, and in ethics. In 1904
and 1905, Duhem advanced his philosophical views in articles that
he later brought together in his influential book *La théorie physique:
son objet et sa structure* (1906). In that work he declared, "An experiment in physics can never condemn an isolated hypothesis but only
a whole theoretical group,"[1] and his reference to a whole theoretical
group led later writers to call Duhem's view holistic or corporatistic.
According to Duhem, a physicist who carries out an experiment, or
gives a report of the results of one, implicitly accepts the accuracy
of a conjunction of hypotheses. To show this, Duhem considered
the case in which a physicist calls a law into question. How does he
justify his doubts? asked Duhem. Some would say that he deduces

---

[1] Pierre Duhem, *The Aim and Structure of Physical Theory*, trans. Philip P. Wiener (Princeton, 1954), p. 183. This edition is hereafter cited parenthetically in the text.

a prediction from the law, observes whether the predicted event occurs, and rejects the law if it does not. But, Duhem insisted, when
the physicist deduces his prediction, he deduces it from more than
the isolated law; and therefore if the predicted phenomenon does
not occur, the whole conjunction of statements used by the physicist
is at fault. According to Duhem, "The only thing the experiment
teaches us is that among the propositions used to predict the phenomenon and to establish whether it would be produced, there is at
least one error; but where this error lies is just what it does not tell
us. The physicist may declare that this error is contained in exactly
the proposition he wishes to refute, but is he sure it is not in another
proposition? If he is, he accepts implicitly the accuracy of all the
other propositions he has used" (p. 185).

Duhem adds that when a whole theory or conjunction faces what
Quine calls a recalcitrant experience, the physicist has no absolute
principle that tells him how to repair the conjunction. One physicist
may safeguard his fundamental hypotheses by adding complications
to his total theory, whereas another physicist, who disdains what he
regards as excessively complicated artificial procedures, may decide
to change one of his fundamental hypotheses. A physicist may prefer
one or the other of such revisions, not because it is dictated by what
Duhem called pure logic but because he is governed by "reasons
which reason does not know," reasons of good sense that do not
impose themselves with the same implacable rigor that the prescriptions of logic do (p. 217). Duhem distinguishes between the statements of physics, the prescriptions of logic, and his reasons of good
sense. Although he says that a physicist who rejects a total theory
because it has been refuted by an experiment uses a mode of demon-
stration that seems to be as irrefutable as a mathematician's proof
by reduction to absurdity, Duhem points out that a refuted physical
theory implies a false contingent statement about nature whereas
a mathematical theory that is reduced to absurdity implies a self-
contradictory statement (p. 185). Insofar as Duhem distinguished

sharply between logico-mathematical statements and contingent statements about nature, his philosophy contained vestiges of rationalism; and insofar as he appealed to reasons that reason does not know, he appealed to considerations having to do with the elegance or simplicity of a conjunction of statements.

Duhem's holism was influenced by the historicism and the organicism of the nineteenth century. He was a distinguished student of the history of science and his organicism led him to write: "Physics is not a machine which lets itself be taken apart; we cannot try each piece in isolation and, in order to adjust it, wait until its solidity has been carefully checked." Physical science "is an organism in which one part cannot be made to function except when the parts that are most remote from it are called into play, some more so than others, but all to some degree" (pp. 187–88). Duhem adds that if some discomfort is felt in the functioning of this organism, the physicist will have to go through the entire system to see which organ needs to be remedied or modified without being able to isolate any organ and examine it alone. By contrast, the watchmaker who tries to fix a watch that has stopped separates all the wheel works and examines them one by one until he finds the part that is defective or broken. Another diagnostician, the doctor, cannot dissect a patient in order to establish a diagnosis, and so he has to guess at the cause of the ailment by examining the disorders affecting the whole body. The physicist, Duhem says, is more like a doctor than a watchmaker.

A few years after Duhem advanced his view of scientific confirmation, Bertrand Russell extended it in an essay titled "Pragmatism" that appeared in 1909, an essay in which he discusses the views of William James. In an almost forgotten part of his essay, Russell attributed to James a version of holism like that advocated by Tarski and Quine about forty years later—a holism that included the truths of mathematics in the totality of beliefs that are tested by experience or facts. Below I quote the passage in which Russell expounds and applauds this view while examining the ideas of James. It is also of interest because it shows that Russell once subscribed to a variety of epistemological holism that contradicted the view of the relation between pure mathematics and natural science that he accepted at other times during his long life.

Russell writes:

> One of the approaches to pragmatism is through the consideration of induction and scientific method. The old inductive philosophy, as exemplified in Mill's logic, conceived the nature and scope of induction far too narrowly, and pragmatism deserves credit for having remedied this defect. Induction, though it cannot give complete certainty, underlies all the sciences, even pure mathematics. In any science, we have a collection of facts bound together (as far as possible) by general laws. The facts appear, in the formal exposition, as deductions from the laws; this, at least, holds for the most advanced sciences, such as mathematics and physics. But in reality the laws are inductions from the facts. We cannot say that this or that fact proves this or that law: the whole body of facts proves (or, rather, renders probable) the whole body of laws. It might be thought that, in an *experimentum crucis*, a single fact establishes a single law; but this is only the case so long as the other laws of the science are taken for granted. If other facts should lead us to doubt the other laws, the interpretation of our *experimentum crucis* might be wholly changed. Thus the justification of a science is that it fits all the known facts, and that no alternative system of hypotheses is known which fits the facts equally well.[2]

This passage shows that in addition to accepting a philosophy of induction that he attributes to pragmatism, Russell says that induction, which "cannot give complete certainty," underlies *pure* mathematics—a position that obviously runs counter to some of his later views. Russell also maintains here that we cannot say that this or that fact proves this or that law of the most advanced sciences "such as mathematics and physics" but rather must say that "the whole body of facts proves (or, rather, renders probable) the whole body

---

[2] Bertrand Russell, *Philosophical Essays* (London, 1910), pp. 104–5.

of laws." In support of this holistic view, Russell denies that a single fact in a crucial experiment establishes a single law. His objection is that this is true only so long as the other laws of the science are taken for granted, an objection made a few years earlier by Duhem in a section of his *Aim and Structure of Physical Theory* titled "A 'Crucial Experiment' Is Impossible in Physics."

Duhem considers an attempt to show by what is called Foucault's experiment that Newton's hypothesis that light consists of tiny corpuscles or particles should be rejected in favor of Huygens's hypothesis that light consists of waves. Both of these theories explain a number of light's properties; but Newton's hypothesis implies that light travels faster in water than in air, whereas Huygens's hypothesis implies that it travels faster in air than in water. The physicist Jean Foucault supposedly showed that light travels faster in air; so, in accordance with the theory of crucial experiments, the victory allegedly went to Huygens and the wave theory while the corpuscular theory of Newton was rejected. At this point Duhem steps in with his holism and asserts that Foucault's conclusion was not derived from Newton's hypothesis *alone*, but from a conjunction of that hypothesis and certain other assumptions. Therefore, Duhem argues, Foucault's conclusion that light does not travel faster in water does not imply that Newton's hypothesis is false; rather, it implies that the conjunction of Newton's hypothesis and other assumptions is false. Thus if one gives the palm to Huygens's wave theory, one must recognize that one is taking for granted the assumptions made by Foucault, which is the sort of thing Russell had in mind when he asserted that a so-called crucial experiment may be said to establish a single law only so long as other laws of science are taken for granted.

However, Russell's version of holism was different from Duhem's because Russell included truths of mathematics in the body of laws that faces Russell's facts. In the very section in which Duhem criticizes the idea of a crucial experiment, he is at pains to say that even if using it were to lead to the rejection of one of the two competing theories of light—say, Newton's—that would not permit us to say that the other theory, Huygens's, was a "demonstrated truth" (p. 190). Duhem insists on this because he distinguishes, as we have seen, between the method of "experimental contradiction" and the method of *reductio ad absurdum* used by Euclid, advocating a view that is not compatible with Russell's remark that the laws of pure mathematics are in the whole body of laws that is rendered probable by the whole body of facts. We thus may sum up the views of Duhem, Russell, and James at the turn of the twentieth century as follows: Duhem *did not* include the laws of mathematics in the body of laws that are tested by facts or experience; Russell *did* include them; and James wobbled on the issue in spite of what Russell said about the pragmatic view of induction in the passage I have just quoted. Although James said our beliefs are combined in a stock that faces experience, he distinguished sharply in some parts of *Pragmatism* between truths about matters of fact and those about relations among ideas even though he also speaks of the plasticity of logical and mathematical ideas. In advocating something like Russell's holism of 1909 many years later, Quine and Tarski called into question the positivistic distinction between logical and physical truths by maintaining that even a logical truth *can be* surrendered in the face of a recalcitrant sensory experience, while Quine, Goodman, and I questioned the view that the truths of philosophy or essential predications are analytic. Furthermore, the psychologism of Tarski and Quine when they rejected rationalism[3] supports the view that philosophers may talk empirically about science and other aspects of culture, and it diverges from the view that philosophy asserts only analytic propositions.

This combination of psychologism and holism also diverges from Carnap's view that "the only proper task of *Philosophy* is *Logical Anal-*

---

[3] See Morton White, ed., "A Philosophical Letter of Alfred Tarski," *Journal of Philosophy* 84 (1987): 28–32; Tarski remarks in this letter of 1944 that his willingness to reject a logical axiom is a psychological matter. And in *The Pursuit of Truth* (Cambridge, Mass., 1990), p. 19, for example, Quine maintains that epistemology is a branch of psychology.

ysis" and that "the function of logical analysis is to analyze all knowledge, all assertions of science and of everyday life, in order to make
clear the sense of each such assertion and the connections between
them."[4] According to Carnap, neither art nor religion is a proper
concern of philosophy: he says at one point that "only the propositions of mathematics and empirical science have sense." And since
he thinks the task of the philosopher is to analyze the sense of propositions in those domains, he implies that neither music, poetry, nor
religion provides the philosopher with material about which to philosophize; he also speaks of the "non-theoretical character of the
arts."[5] Furthermore, Carnap, like Lewis, makes a sharp distinction
between logical analytic propositions that are not empirical and scientific synthetic propositions that are, and he seems to hold that the
propositions of ontology are not empirical. It was against such a
view of philosophy and against such a sharp distinction between the
analytic and the synthetic that Tarski and Quine reacted.[6] They
rested some of their opposing arguments on the holistic view that
logical principles are components of conjunctions that are tested
empirically. They regarded some of their own philosophical assertions about science as empirical, seeing themselves as psychological
or anthropological students of it.

Their view also challenged a conception of analytic philosophy
sponsored by G. E. Moore. In his *Principia Ethica* of 1903 Moore
insisted on the difference between analyzing a property such as
being good and saying that it applies to all and only things that
have another property. It was such a view that underlay the attack
of Moore and Russell against what they took to be James's theory
that "true" means the same as "useful". When Moore later tried to
elucidate his notion of philosophical analysis, he maintained that
when one gives an analysis of a concept such as being a brother, the

---

[4] Rudolf Carnap, *Philosophy and Logical Syntax* (London, 1935), pp. 35, 9–10.

[5] Ibid., pp. 36, 31.

[6] See W. V. Quine, "Two Dogmas of Empiricism," in *From a Logical Point of View: Nine Logico-Philosophical Essays* (Cambridge, 1953), pp. 20–46; originally published in *Philosophical Review* 60 (January 1951). Also see Tarski, "Philosophical Letter."

term that expresses the concept analyzed—the *analysandum*—must be synonymous with the analyzing term, the *analysans*. And when he said that the statement in which one offers an analysis by saying something like "To be a brother is to be a male sibling" must be analytic rather than synthetic, he continued the tradition of those who maintained that the statement "All and only men are rational animals" is analytic whereas "All and only men have opposable thumbs" is synthetic. However, Moore was typically candid in saying, "The line between 'analytic' and 'synthetic' might be drawn in many different ways. As it is, I do not think that the two terms have any clear meaning."[7] It followed, of course, that Moore's own notion of analysis lacked clarity; and if the notion of the analytic is itself unclear and it lacks a clear criterion, the supposedly sharp distinction between analytic philosophy and empirical science becomes problematic, to say the least.

The tendency to regard philosophical statements of synonymy as empirical has bearing on the view that every logical principle is immune to rejection by experience. By contrast, Tarski and Quine held that some logical principles *can be* rejected when a theory of which they are conjuncts is confronted by a recalcitrant experience (though we rarely reject logical principles because of their age and their generality, as Mill and Tarski said, and as James suggested at places). As we shall see later, it does not follow that according to holistic pragmatists we may reject every logical principle, especially those we use when we employ the hypothetico-deductive method. In this connection I have called attention not only to Carnap's view that logical principles are immune to refutation by experience, but also to Moore's view that the philosopher often analyzes concepts by asserting analytic truths. If Moore had been asked how he knows that to be a brother is to be a male sibling, he would have replied that he knows this by virtue of an analysis of the concept or attribute of being a brother, which is stated in a proposition that is tested

---

[7] G. E. Moore, "A Reply to My Critics," in *The Philosophy of G. E. Moore*, ed. Paul Arthur Schilpp (Evanston, Ill., 1942), p. 667.

not by experience but rather by seeing an identity of attributes. By contrast, holists avoid talk about attributes for they base their analyses on the synonymy of linguistic expressions, and their enterprise would be empirical if a criterion of synonymy were available. Such a study would be psychological in nature and would be consonant with the broader empirical view of philosophy that governed the work of William James on religion and that of John Dewey on art.

Having called Duhem a forerunner of pragmatic holism, I want to say something in this connection about the later Wittgenstein. Like Moore before him, Wittgenstein was interested in ordinary language, but unlike Moore he was not given to saying that an expression like "brother" expressed an abstract concept or attribute. Instead of holding that the task of philosophy is to analyze Platonic attributes or meanings, Wittgenstein said that the meaning of a linguistic expression is its use and that the main task of philosophy is to study the behavior of human beings who use language in many different ways. In my opinion, this constituted a link between his philosophy and that of psychologically oriented pragmatists, especially with William James. Like James he was interested in why men philosophize; like John Dewey he was concerned to study social linguistic behavior; like epistemological holists he thought that linguistic expressions are embedded in what he called a "Lebensform" or "form of life". "To imagine a language," he says, "means to imagine a form of life" and "the *speaking* of language is part of an activity, or of a form of life."[8]

Wittgenstein encouraged philosophers to recognize that man does not communicate by assertion and proof alone, since man tells stories, greets, exclaims, exhorts, commands, judges, describes, promises, and does many other things with words. Therefore all of these linguistic activities are fair game for the philosopher who abandons the Mooreian idea that philosophers seek to analyze only attributes or concepts, and it calls into question the view that the

[8] Ludwig Wittgenstein, *Philosophical Investigations*, trans. G. E. M. Anscombe (Oxford, 1978), secs. 19, 23 (pp. 8, 11).

philosopher is interested only in the logical analysis of scientific statements. According to my understanding of Wittgenstein's later views, a philosopher may study the language men use in the writing of history, in morality, law, religion, politics, and education; and a philosopher may compare and contrast language as it is used for purposes of communication within all of these different institutions. While communicating, men use language in a variety of intertwined ways that express their beliefs, their hopes, their needs, and their values; and one job of the philosopher is to describe the interconnections among these different modes of speech, feeling, and thought. I believe therefore that the later philosophy of Wittgenstein encouraged an expansive view of philosophy as the philosophy of culture as well as a holistic pragmatism, but I must add a qualification. Although his view that philosophers should study how we use language and his view that using it is a form of life are compatible with a pragmatic holism that permits no sharp epistemic distinction between analytic and synthetic statements, he also seems to hold that some statements are factual whereas others are accepted merely on the basis of grammar. Did he accept a sharp dichotomy between analytic and synthetic truth? If he did, then, like James, Dewey, and Duhem, his philosophy contained a vestige of rationalism; but I think he was more of an ally of holistic pragmatism than he is often made out to be, especially when he encouraged philosophers to describe the many uses of language.

Before concluding my discussion of the dualisms of logical empiricism, I want to say something about Hume's distinction between truths supported by "abstract reasoning concerning quantity or number" and those supported by "experimental reasoning concerning matter of fact and existence"[9]—a distinction that is often said to prefigure a basic view of logical empiricism. I believe that in spite of seeming to be an epistemic dualist and a half-rationalist, Hume may not be. Since he stated that arithmetical truths are established

[9] David Hume, *An Inquiry Concerning Human Understanding*, ed. Charles W. Hendel (Indianapolis, 1955), sec. XII, part III (p. 173).

by examining relations between ideas, he might be called a half-rationalist, especially when we compare his views with those of Quine. But when we carefully examine Hume's view that *a priori* or logically necessary truths are established by examining relations between ideas, we may wonder whether he consistently defended a rationalistic view of *a priori* or necessary truth, as a half-rationalist would. Ideas for Hume are psychological entities—weak perceptions, he called them. Therefore they are in certain respects like the concrete particles of Newton and different from the abstract ideas of Plato; indeed, Hume said that they are governed by psychological laws of association much as Newton's particles are governed by his law of gravitation. Hume held that the truth of *a priori* statements depends *entirely* on the ideas related. And because he said that statements expressing four relations depend entirely on ideas—"resemblance, contrariety, degrees in quality, and proportions in quality or number,"[10]—it will be useful to consider a statement that expresses resemblance and should therefore depend entirely on ideas.

D.G.C. MacNabb has tried to elucidate Hume's view by referring to a map of the world in which places are treated as analogues of Hume's ideas.[11] Thus the map-idea of North Dakota resembles that of South Dakota in that both map-ideas are approximately rectangular. Let us now ask whether the rectangularity of the two map-ideas can support a logically necessary truth. MacNabb hesitates to say that it does, but it seems to me that it does not. The statement "My map-idea of North Dakota is rectangular and my map-idea of South Dakota is rectangular" seems just as contingent as "North Dakota is rectangular and South Dakota is rectangular," and for this reason alone cannot be offered in deductive support of a supposedly necessary truth. Indeed, it is hard to see what necessary truth this statement about ideas or weak perceptions could be supposed to

---

[10] David Hume, *A Treatise of Human Nature*, ed. L. A. Selby-Bigge (Oxford, 1888), book I, part III, sec. I (p. 70).

[11] D.G.C. MacNabb, "David Hume," in *The Encyclopedia of Philosophy*, ed. Paul Edwards (New York, 1967), 4:79.

support, which is why Hume's apparent concession to rationalism in his philosophy of mathematics may not have been a real concession. If he held that the test of arithmetical truth is based on a contingent statement about ideas as weak perceptions, then it would seem that Hume undercut his own sharp epistemological distinction between two kinds of truth when he said that truths of mathematics are tested by examining psychological entities.

This undercutting seems to be confirmed in a passage of Hume's *Treatise of Human Nature* where he compares "the necessity, which makes two times two equal to four" with "the necessity . . . which unites causes and effects." True, he says throughout his writings that the statement that two times two is equal to four *is not* established by experience, whereas the statement that under normal circumstances a billiard ball must move when it is struck *is* established by experience. Yet when Hume compares the former necessity with the latter, he says that "as the necessity" of the former "lies only in the act of understanding, by which we consider and compare" the ideas expressed in it, "in like manner the necessity or power, which unites causes and effects, lies in the determination of the mind to pass from the one to the other."[12] Hume seems to say here that arithmetical necessity and causal necessity are both psychological insofar as they both lie in the mind, in which case Hume's psychologistic view of the relations between ideas will not support the sharp distinction between *a priori* necessity and causal necessity that is usually associated with his name. It may therefore make him an unwitting ancestor of philosophers who argue against the sharp distinction between analytic statements rather than of the logical empiricists who have claimed him as their ancestor.[13]

---

[12] Hume, *Treatise*, book I, part III, sec. XIV (p. 166).
[13] See my paper "The Psychologism of Hume and Quine Compared," in *Proceedings of the Twentieth World Congress of Philosophy*, ed. M. D. Gedney, Philosophy Documentation Center (Bowling Green, Ky., 2000), 7:151–59.

VI

Holistic Pragmatism and Natural Science

Tarski and Quine

H AVING DESCRIBED SOME OF THE ROOTS OF HO-
listic pragmatism and having also shown
how it avoids the remnants of rationalism in the philosophies of
Hume, Mill, James, Dewey, and Carnap, I want to show in the following chapters how it encourages the view that philosophy of art,
of religion, of morality, or of other elements of culture is in great
measure a discipline that is epistemically coordinate with philosophy
of natural science. Although early advocates of holistic pragmatism
such as Quine and Tarski were interested primarily in the philosophy of mathematics and natural science, I think we may regard studies of other elements of culture or civilization as holistic. Dewey's
philosophy of art, James's philosophy of religion, some of the work
of Nelson Goodman on art, that of Holmes on law, and that of John
Rawls on politics were prime illustrations of such studies in the
twentieth century that I discuss in later chapters after expanding
here on the holistic pragmatist's view of science.

The holistic pragmatist rejects the Cartesian view that philosophy
can extract the essence of truth, of body, and of mind in an *a priori*
fashion, and he challenges the claim that no mathematical and logical principles can be abandoned in the face of a recalcitrant experi-

ence. He agrees with John Stuart Mill that a principle of formal logic may be surrendered without accepting Mill's view that all such principles are inductively confirmed by investigating our mental states.[1] Holists do not say that logical principles are confirmed in accordance with what Russell characterized as "the old inductive philosophy as exemplified in Mill's logic,"[2] because they think that some logical principles and other statements together imply observation statements that are confirmed by experience. They hold that if a statement reporting an experience is rejected, the whole conjunction that logically implies it may be rejected; they also hold that if a prediction of experience turns out to be false, at least one of the components of the whole conjunction that implies it may be rejected, and that component may be a logical statement unless that logical statement is involved in using the holistic pragmatist's method of testing (a point to be developed later).

Although holistic pragmatism is often associated with the doctrine expounded by Quine in his famous 1951 paper, "Two Dogmas of Empiricism," it was succinctly and clearly advocated in a letter written to me in 1944 by Alfred Tarski. There he wrote: "I am ready to reject certain logical premisses (axioms) of our science in exactly the same circumstances in which I am ready to reject empirical premisses (e.g., physical hypotheses); and I do not think that I am an exception in this respect,"[3] perhaps referring to Quine as someone who agreed with him. The explanation Tarski supplied—that we reject certain hypotheses or scientific theories if we notice their inner inconsistency or their disagreement with individual statements reporting certain experiences—is somewhat reminiscent of James. In *Pragmatism*, James had described the process by which an

[1] J. S. Mill, *A System of Logic, Ratiocinative and Inductive: Being a Connected View of the Principles of Evidence, and the Methods of Scientific Investigation*, ed. J. M. Robson (Toronto, 1973), book II, chap. 7, sec. 5 (1:277).

[2] Bertrand Russell, *Philosophical Essays* (London, 1910), p. 104.

[3] Morton White, ed., "A Philosophical Letter of Alfred Tarski," *Journal of Philosophy* 84 (1987): 31. W. V. Quine's "Two Dogmas of Empiricism," originally published in *Philosophical Review* 51 (January 1951), is reprinted in *From a Logical Point of View: Nine Logico-Philosophical Essays* (Cambridge, 1953), pp. 20–46.

individual settles into *new* opinions by saying that "the individual has a stock of old opinions already, but he meets a new experience that puts them to a strain. Somebody contradicts them; or in a reflective moment he discovers that they contradict each other; or he hears of facts with which they are incompatible." But James added another reason for rejecting an old opinion, namely, that "desires arise in him which [his opinions] cease to satisfy."[4] This last reason may be related to the "goodness for life" that James had regarded as a property of true beliefs in his *Varieties of Religious Experience*, but it disappears from the writings of other pragmatists—except perhaps as reflected in their idea (and James's) that a new opinion or hypothesis may contribute to the overall elegance or simplicity of the conjunction of which it is a component and therefore satisfy their esthetic needs.

After saying that we reject certain hypotheses or scientific theories when we notice an inner inconsistency or a disagreement with reports of certain experiences, Tarski, like Russell in his 1909 essay on pragmatism and like Quine in "Two Dogmas of Empiricism," registers the direct or indirect influence of Duhem by saying, "No such experience can logically compel us to reject the theory: too many additional hypotheses (regarding the 'initial conditions', circumstances of the experiment, instruments used) are always involved. We can practically always save the theory by means of additional hypotheses. But often these additional hypotheses are so involved and 'unnatural' that they make us uncomfortable—we begin to feel an inner need of rejecting the theory or some parts of it, and of replacing it by a new, simpler and more natural theory, which would not require these additional hypotheses".[5] Epicycles in astronomy probably seemed unnatural in a way that led other scientists to seek a new, simpler, and more natural astronomy; and perhaps, as I have said, this virtue of an improved theory is the virtue of

[4] William James, *Pragmatism*, [ed. Fredson Bowers and Ignas K. Skrupskelis] (Cambridge, Mass., 1975), pp. 34–35.
[5] Tarski, "Philosophical Letter," p. 31.

elegance or simplicity mentioned by James. When, however, James added the moral feature of being good for life as a virtue of a theory, some eminent pragmatists dissociated themselves sharply from his version of pragmatism: they thought that an esthetic feature of a scientific belief or theory—its simplicity or elegance—might be an epistemic virtue but that the moral one of contributing to a better life for the believer was not. Both Peirce and Dewey recoiled from that doctrine of James.

Returning to Tarski's holism, I come now to that part of his letter in which he says that a conflict with a report of experience may lead us to reject a special law that is an inductive generalization or a more general hypothesis, or even one of the fundamental principles of our science like Newton's theory of universal gravitation. Tarski then adds: "Axioms of logic are of so general a nature that they are rarely affected by such experiences in special domains. However, I don't see here any difference 'of principle'; I can imagine that certain new experiences of a very fundamental nature may make us inclined to change *just some* [my emphasis] axioms of logic. And certain new developments in quantum mechanics seem clearly to indicate this possibility. That we are reluctant to do so is beyond any doubts; after all, 'logical truths' are not only more general, but also much older than physical theories or even geometrical axioms. And perhaps we single out these logically true sentences, combine them in a class, just to express our reluctance to reject them." After presenting this summary of his holism, Tarski makes another significant comment: "Whether this description is true and adequate—I don't know. I have the impression that many people would agree with it." I lay special emphasis on Tarski's calling what he says a "description," for it echoes his statement that the main problem he deals with here is "of a psychological character."[6] Tarski thinks his reflections fall into the domain of psychology considered as a descriptive science, and so he not only adopts an empiricist view of logical truths

---

[6] Ibid., pp. 31–32.

insofar as he thinks some of them may be abandoned in the light of a recalcitrant experience but also thinks that what he says *about* the role of logical truths in science is descriptive and empirical. He not only abandons the view that no principle of logic can be surrendered in the face of experience, but he also abandons the view that no statement in the philosophy or psychology of science can be refuted by appealing to experience. I might add in passing that this view departs from Wittgenstein's position in his *Tractatus Logico-Philosophicus* that "philosophy is not one of the natural sciences" and that "psychology is no more closely related to philosophy than any other natural science."[7] It also departs from the view in the *Tractatus* that the statements of philosophy are senseless, and for all of these reasons it is consonant with the view that the philosophy of science is a discipline that is coordinate with the philosophy of art, religion, law, history, and politics.

Because rationalists like Descartes held that metaphysical statements such as "No body is a mind" are established by pure reason just as mathematical statements are, I turn now from the status of logical principles to the status of so-called essential predications like "Every man is a rational animal." If we regard the formal principle of logic "Every *P* is *P*" as a logical truth, we may also regard "Every man is a man" as a logical truth because it is deduced from "Every *P* is *P*" merely by substituting constants for variables in a logical truth. We may then replace the second occurrence of "man" in "Every man is a man" by the expression "rational animal", which is supposedly synonymous with "man", and deduce "Every man is a rational animal" from "Every man is a man" and ultimately from "Every *P* is *P*". We may now say that "Every man is a rational animal" is analytic, whereas "Every man is a featherless biped" is synthetic because "man" is not synonymous with "featherless biped". If we maintain that the substitution of constants for variables *and* the replacement

---

[7] Ludwig Wittgenstein, *Tractatus Logico-Philosophicus*, trans. C. K. Ogden (London, 1933), 4.111, 4.1121 (pp. 75–77).

of synonyms for synonyms both preserve *logical truth*, then we may say that "Every man is a rational animal" is a logical truth.

Now we may say, as Tarski and Quine do, that this logical truth is at the mercy of experience because it is a component of a large conjunction of truths that we may deny if that conjunction leads to false predictions of experience. In that case the epistemic status of "Every man is a rational animal" is no different from that of "Every man is a featherless biped." Furthermore, we may point out that the deduction of the supposedly analytic statement "Every man is a rational animal" from "Every *P* is *P*" depends on asserting that "man" is synonymous with "rational animal", which is empirical inasmuch as it says something descriptive about language. So, even if we should think that "Every *P* is *P*" is *not* established by experience, our claim that "Every man is a rational animal" is analytic is supported by saying that it is deduced from "Every *P* is *P*" with the help of an empirical statement of synonymy. Moreover, our derivation of the analyticity of "Every man is a rational animal" by assuming an empirical statement of synonymy is *not* based on an arbitrary definition of "man" as short for "rational animal". If "Every man is a rational animal" were a logical consequence of "Every man is a man" merely because of an arbitrary convention that "man" is short for "rational animal", then someone who instead treated "man" as short for "featherless biped" could legitimately regard "Every man is a featherless biped" as analytic. Such relativistic conventionalism does not reflect what essentialists usually say when distinguishing essential from accidental predications, for they rest attributions of essentialness or analyticity on what they call "real definitions" that are nonconventional statements of synonymy.

If the difference between "Every man is a rational animal" and "Every man is a featherless biped" is based on the synonymy of "man" and "rational animal" and on the nonsynonymy of "man" and "featherless biped", the question arises: How do we establish such synonymy or nonsynonymy? Some philosophers, such as Mill,

Moore, Russell, and C. I. Lewis, said that the word "man" and the expression "rational animal" both express the same attribute, where an attribute is the sense or connotation of a predicate as opposed to its denotation—something that we have in mind when applying the word "man" to an object. This is the doctrine that Russell and Moore confidently assumed when they criticized what they took to be James's view of truth. They accused James of conflating the denotation of "true" with its connotation when he said that it means the same as "useful"; they treated him as though he were saying that the concept or attribute of being true is identical with the concept or attribute of being useful. But now we may ask Moore and Russell: How do we know that the attribute of being true is not the same as that of being useful? When Mill tried to answer a related question about the relation between the attribute of being a man and that of being rational, he said of philosophers who maintained that *man* cannot be conceived without *rationality* that "all which is really true" in their assertion "is only that if he had not rationality, he would not be reputed a man." However, Mill also said that the distinction he drew between an essential and an accidental predication "corresponds to that which is drawn by Kant and other metaphysicians between what they term *analytic* and *synthetic* judgments; the former being those which can be evolved from the meaning of the terms used".[8] This suggests that Mill was speaking of a relation between meanings or concepts when dealing with essential predication.

It is worth pointing out that Mill seems to approach this subject in two different ways. According to one, the extralinguistic entity that is the meaning of the word "man"—the attribute of being a man—*involves* the attribute of being rational; but after saying this, he tells us little that is helpful about that relation of involvement. Mill does not provide a criterion of involvement; he does not elucidate the difference between involvement and noninvolvement that underlies his distinction between essential and nonessential predica-

---

[8] Mill, *Logic*, book I, chap. 6, secs. 2, 4 (1:111, 116).

tion or the related one of Kant between analytic and synthetic predication. He is therefore reduced to saying that one merely sees that
one attribute involves another, much as Moore, Russell, and C. I.
Lewis said later. A second approach that Mill takes is not based explicitly on the relation of involvement of attributes; rather it relies
on the linguistic fact that we do not apply the word "man" to individuals who lack the attribute of rationality. A more thoroughly linguistic form of this view would be that as a matter of fact we apply
the word "man" to an individual if and only if we apply the expression "rational animal" to that individual. This view resembles the
view that the synonymy of "man" and "rational animal" is factual:
we apply the first expression to an individual if and only if we apply
the other, something that presumably can be established only by
examining what speakers do. Since it seems paradoxical to some to
say that an analytic truth such as "Every man is a rational animal"
is shown to be analytic and therefore necessary by asserting a contingent synthetic empirical proposition about linguistic habits, it might
be argued that Mill's other view—the view that we show the analyticity of "Every man is a rational animal" by asserting that the attribute of being a man is identical with the attribute of being a rational
animal, and the converse—is preferable. Even then, however, we are
left with a paradox. Saying that the sentence "Every man is a rational
animal" is analytic requires us to say not only that the attribute of
being a man is identical with being a rational animal, but also that
the linguistic expression "man" connotes the attribute of being a
man and that the linguistic expression "rational animal" connotes
the attribute of being a rational animal; and these last two statements
about connoting are empirical because it is a contingent empirical
truth that an expression in English happens to connote a certain
attribute.

   The question therefore arises: Do we need to refer at all to attributes in order to establish synonymy and analyticity? Quine thinks
we do not, and once argued that we should instead seek a behavioristic criterion for synonymy that avoids such a reference because there

is no criterion for the identity of attributes. However, no behavioristic criterion for synonymy emerged in the half century or so that has passed since he first began to seek one, and so he and others abandoned the search. It should be borne in mind that an empirical criterion of synonymy would stand to it just as a constant associated with the metal iron stands to iron. The physicist says, for example, that if and only if a thing has a stretch modulus of 19×10 dynes per square centimeter is it iron, and Quine's search was based on the hope that we could show that a given expression is synonymous with another just as a physicist shows that a thing is iron by pointing out that it has a certain stretch modulus. It might seem that this criterion could be given by saying, as Mill seems to say, that "man" and "rational animal" are synonymous if and only we apply the predicate "man" to an individual just in case we apply the predicate "rational animal" to that individual. But since it might also be said that we apply "man" to an individual just in case we apply "featherless biped" to that individual, we could not say that "All men are rational animals" is analytic whereas "All men are featherless bipeds" is synthetic. In response, as we have seen, some philosophers maintain that the only way in which a sharp distinction can be drawn is by saying that two predicates are synonymous if and only if what we have in mind when applying one predicate—say, the attribute of being a man, to Socrates—is the same as what we have in mind when applying the other predicate—the attribute or concept of being a rational animal to Socrates. But how can we know what attribute another person has in mind? And how does *she* know that she has the same attribute in mind when she says that being a man is being the same as being a rational animal?

   All of this tended to favor an approach once sketched by Nelson Goodman when he abandoned the effort to find a criterion for synonymy that would make the distinction between analytic and synthetic sharp. He maintained at one time that a philosopher or scientist who says that the predicate "rational animal" is synonymous with "man", whereas "featherless biped" is not, thinks in the light of empirical evidence that "rational animal" is less likely to differ in extension from "man" than "featherless biped" is.[9] Goodman believed this to be superior to a criterion that expressed a concept, a meaning, or an attribute in mind, inasmuch as it refers to the publicly observable linguistic habits of human beings. His approach resembled one of Mill's; unlike Mill, however, Goodman thought the philosopher's statement " 'Every man is a rational animal' is analytic but 'Every man is a featherless biped' is synthetic" should be abandoned, perhaps in favor of saying something like " 'Every man is a rational animal' is very analytic but 'Every man is a featherless biped' is less analytic." It should be noted that statements traditionally regarded as analytic might on this view change from being analytic to being synthetic or vice versa. In response to anyone who regarded this as an objection, Goodman maintained that the extension of "analytic" as used by philosophers was a wavering one and that he had no reliable pre-philosophical beliefs that led him to say whether a given sentence was or was not analytic. He maintained therefore that his version of the distinction between analytic and synthetic came as close as he could come to the traditional extensions of those terms; thus he gave up the effort to produce a clear distinction that would result in sharply distinguishing analytic sheep from synthetic goats. Goodman's distinction is obviously a psychological one that leads to our regarding "analytic" and "synthetic" as empirical terms. Furthermore, when Goodman says that "Every man is a rational animal" is very analytic, he treats it much as Tarski and Quine treat some logical statements when they say that we are very reluctant to surrender them. Both views are in accord with James's idea that there are some beliefs in our stock—some logical, some not—that we are highly reluctant to surrender when a novel

---

[9] See Nelson Goodman, W. V. Quine, and Morton White, "A Triangular Correspondence in 1947," appendix to *A Philosopher's Story*, by Morton White (University Park, Pa., 1999), pp. 337–57.

experience calls the whole stock into question, as well as with Russell's holistic interpretation of the pragmatic view of induction mentioned in chapter 5.

I want to emphasize that the pragmatic holist not only regards logical and nonlogical statements as components of conjunctions that are tested empirically, he also regards some statements *about* them in epistemology as empirical. In addition, he treats ontology as a part of empirical science, because he thinks that there is no sharp epistemic distinction between an ontological statement like "There are physical objects" and a physical statement like "There are electrons"; both are at the mercy of experience insofar as they are components of holistic conjunctions that are tested by experience. That is why I believe that holistic pragmatism paves the way for regarding art, religion, history, law, and politics as institutions that may also be studied by the philosopher of culture. I shall argue later that moral thinking may also be treated holistically, as Rawls did as well, thereby taking holism farther than Quine was willing to extend it. In my view an ethical principle may be tested as a component of a holistic conjunction that works a manageable structure into a flux of experience once we recognize that that flux contains moral feelings of obligation as well as sensory experiences. In the remaining chapters, therefore, I show how the philosophy of history, of art, of law, and of politics may also be viewed in this way, thereby continuing a tradition defended in James's *Varieties of Religious Experience* and also in Dewey's *Art as Experience* despite their occasional concessions to rationalism.

VII

Holistic Pragmatism and the Philosophy of History

LTHOUGH THE ORIGIN OF HOLISTIC PRAGMATISM is often located in the writings of Duhem, it is fair to say that a germ of it is present in the so-called regularity or covering law theory of explanation espoused much earlier by Hume and Mill. As we have seen, one of the main tenets of holistic pragmatism is that scientists test conjunctions of statements rather than isolated statements, whereas the main tenet of the regularity theory is that a singular causal or explanatory statement that Socrates died because he drank hemlock is established by showing that everyone who drinks hemlock soon dies, that Socrates drank hemlock at a certain time, and that therefore Socrates died soon afterward. Here we do not support our singular causal statement by itself unless we hold the dubious view that we can directly see a causal connection between Socrates' drinking hemlock and his dying without appealing to any general truths. Instead, according to the regularity theory, we support it by appealing to a well-confirmed conjunction of statements—one universal, the others singular—which is what makes our argument a simple holistic one.

In the middle of the twentieth century, the regularity theory of causal explanation advanced by Hume and Mill was carefully developed by Carl G. Hempel and Karl Popper, both of whom applied it to historical explanation.[1] Their investigations were typical of work carried out by logically oriented philosophers of history, investigations that differed dramatically from the theorizing of Vico, Hegel, and Marx in earlier centuries. Because historical speculation was attacked in the twentieth century for employing such dubious notions as the World Spirit and for lacking empirical support, its reputation declined sharply among British and American philosophers who abandoned neo-Hegelian idealism and who came to look down on what the Oxford epistemologist H. H. Price once called the dreary subject of *Kulturphilosophie*. Even when Quine tried to blur the supposed boundary between speculative metaphysics and natural science by accepting on empirical grounds the existence of the sets needed by classical mathematics,[2] he certainly did not seek to inspire interest in historical speculation. So, for a variety of reasons, the preoccupation of Vico, Hegel, Comte, and Marx with the cycles or stages through which societies go took a back seat to interest in the method of historical inquiry. Isaiah Berlin, staunch admirer of Vico that he was, had little sympathy for Vico's obsession with triads or with his parallels between the patterns of rise, apogee, and fall of civilizations, calling Vico's speculative theory "the first in a series of fanciful constructions which culminate in the morphologies of history of Saint-Simon, Fourier, Comte, Ballanche, Spengler, Sorokin, Toynbee"[3]—a group of thinkers who did not fill Berlin with admiration. However, while many twentieth-century philosophers of history dissociated themselves from those constructions, their interest in historical method should not be confused with the professional historian's technical interest in the tools of textual criticism, in the method of dating coins and documents, or in the establishment of authorship. So-called analytic, critical, and linguistic philosophers

[1] See C. G. Hempel, "The Function of General Laws in History," *Journal of Philosophy* 39 (1942): 35–48; Karl Popper, *The Open Society and Its Enemies* (London, 1945), 2:chap. 25, sec. 2.

[2] W. V. Quine, "Two Dogmas of Empiricism," in *From a Logical Point of View: Nine Logico-Philosophical Essays* (Cambridge, 1953), p. 20.

[3] Isaiah Berlin, *Vico and Herder: Two Studies in the History of Ideas* (New York, 1976), p. 68.

of history are more concerned with the role of general statements in historical explanation and the role that the historian's interest plays when a narrative is presented.

One of the primary aims of the historian is to tell a story that is mainly concerned with a group of persons and in the case of biography with one; and sometimes he writes a history of a belief or of a set of beliefs. That distinguishes the historian's task from that of the physicist, whose main aim is to present theories and laws; it also distinguishes it from that of the moralist, who tries to guide and justify action by citing moral principles and singular statements of fact. The historian's causal explanations usually rely on laws or generalizations that are far less speculative than those advanced by Hegel and Marx, generalizations that appear in sciences like psychology, sociology, and economics or in that informal discipline or institution called common sense. Furthermore, it is the historian's interest that determines the selection of what is to be explained and what explains it. One of the main tasks of the critical or analytic philosophy of history, therefore, is to say how generalization—whether homemade by the historian or borrowed from other disciplines—plays a part in historical explanation, and how a historian's judgments of importance or interest operate in the construction of a narrative. The historian seeks to tell the truth as natural and social scientists do, but his main aim is not to generalize. When telling a story, he is concerned with what Alcibiades did and suffered, as Aristotle said, or with what a group of people did and suffered—but telling a story about Alcibiades or the Greek people is not a matter of writing or uttering a short sentence of the kind that might appear on a gravestone. Telling a story is writing or uttering a comparatively long conjunction of interconnected causal statements that depend on general statements and that focus on the doings of a person or of a group of persons in an effort to show how that person or group developed from an earlier stage.

A history, like a scientific theory, should lead logically to statements that can be confirmed by experience, whereas a theoretical scientist who accepts the kinetic theory of gases or Newton's law of gravitation takes deductive steps when deriving less general laws while en route to testing by experience. In the course of a narrative, the historian typically says that because Japan lacked foodstuffs at the beginning of the Meiji era, it became a maritime nation; but when the physicist says that Boyle's Law is true because the kinetic theory of gases is, the physicist usually intends to assert a deductive relation rather than a relation of causal efficacy between the theory and the law—to assert that the law can be deduced from the kinetic theory and other statements. Yet, though the historian does not deduce the singular statement that Japan became a maritime nation directly from the singular statement that it lacked foodstuffs, general truths may play a part in his thinking. When attempting to defend the singular causal statement that links these two statements, the historian may do so by deducing the statement that Japan became a maritime nation from the statement that it lacked foodstuffs and a general statement, thereby supporting it by means of a miniature Duhemian conjunction.

Generalization and Historical Explanation

If a historian says that a singular causal statement is true if and only if there is a general statement linking Japan's lacking food in the Meiji era and Japan's becoming a maritime nation, he may be asked to specify that general statement. One temptation is to answer that the relevant law or general statement is "Whenever a nation lacks a steady supply of food, it becomes a maritime nation," but such a simple generalization is often false, as it is in this case. That is why, when Arnold Toynbee maintained that Holland became a prosperous nation merely because it was responding to the challenge of the sea, his Dutch critic Pieter Geyl replied that we cannot attribute Holland's prosperity simply to the challenge of the sea, because the alleged law, "Whenever a nation is challenged by the sea, it prospers," is false as it stands.[4] Geyl's point was that other events and circumstances combined with the sea's challenge to produce Holland's success: for example, its excellent soil, the expertise in dyke building that it had learned from the Romans, and the excellent maritime situation created by its great ports. This point committed Geyl to accepting the more complex generalization: "Whenever a nation is challenged by the sea, *and* it has excellent soil, *and* it is expert at dyke building, *and* it has an excellent maritime situation, it prospers."

But suppose that this enlarged generalization also turns out to be false. In that case, Geyl would probably search for still other factors that would turn it into a true generalization if he were confident that the combination of factors first mentioned by him were partly responsible for Holland's success. If Geyl knew what the missing factors were, he would be able to present a full-fledged deductive explanation; but how would Geyl know that *there is* such a full-fledged explanation if he could not produce these supplementary factors? How does he know that *there are* other features of Holland that, together with the features he mentions, constitute what Mill called the whole cause of Holland's prosperity? Even to say that certain factors are partial or contributing causes, he must know that *there is* a whole cause of which they are parts, and so the question arises: How does Geyl show that *there is* a whole cause and therefore that *there is* a general truth of the kind that he needs if he cannot say what that general truth is? He may attempt to do this by adducing statistical evidence that justifies his saying that there is such a law. Medical doctors frequently make such an inference from statistical evidence to the assertion that there is a causal connection between taking a certain medicine and curing a disease, and I think historians do something similar when they present explanations that rest on statistical correlations even though they may not be as likely as medical researchers to present those correlations.

[4] Pieter Geyl, "Toynbee's System of Civilizations," in *Toynbee and History: Critical Essays and Reviews*, ed. M. F. Ashley Montagu (Boston, 1956), pp. 46–47.

Since I have discussed this question at length in another place,[5] I will be comparatively brief here. First of all, we must recognize that it is very difficult to support a statement that there is an explanation of a certain kind if we cannot produce such an explanation. If I say "Someone hates John," I can support my statement by mentioning Jane, who hates him. But when I cannot mention a particular person who hates John and yet persist in saying that someone hates him, I am in a tight spot. Of course, I may give up my statement that someone hates John, and the counterpart to this would be to recant my statement that *there is* a conjunction of factors and a general truth that constitute a full-fledged explanation of Holland's prosperity. But, as I have said, even if the historian claims to present a *partial* or *contributory* cause instead of the whole cause of Holland's prosperity, he implies that there is a general truth that links all the contributory or partial causes with Holland's success. Philosophers who find this situation disturbing may respond differently. Some say that the trouble lies in the requirement that the generalization in a full-fledged explanation be universal, such as "*Whenever* a nation is challenged by the sea, and it has excellent soil, and it is expert at dyke building, and it has an excellent maritime situation, it prospers." Instead, they say, the supporting generalization need only begin with the words "Usually when" instead of "Whenever"—the historian need only produce or assert the existence of an explanatory argument whose major premise asserts a high probability. To this other philosophers reply that using a statistical generalization as a premise will not do, because Holland may have been one of the cases that the statistical generalization does not cover—and so, if we want to know what explains *Holland's* prosperity, we should not be satisfied by talk about what is true for the most part. An appeal to statistical regularity will not satisfy these philosophers; only the production of a strict regularity will suffice.

---

[5] See Morton White, *Foundations of Historical Knowledge* (New York, 1965), esp. chaps. 2, 3, and 4. Throughout this chapter I have drawn freely on what I have said in that earlier work, and I have also tried to improve what I said there.

In reaction to such a criticism of the regularity theory, some philosophers have argued that we should abandon it altogether because it just doesn't fit history; they hold that it is a mistake to try to squeeze history into a Procrustean bed made for natural science. While rejecting a regularity theory of historical explanation, R. G. Collingwood said that all history is the history of human thought.[6] He admitted that natural science, which he contrasted with history, explains a particular piece of litmus paper's turning pink by saying that all pieces of litmus paper that are dipped in acid turn pink, and also saying that the particular piece of paper was dipped in acid. But, according to Collingwood, when a historian asks why Brutus stabbed Caesar, the question he means to ask is "What did Brutus think which made him decide to stab Caesar?"; and this, Collingwood also says, cannot be answered in accordance with the regularity theory of explanation. Unfortunately, however, Collingwood oscillates when he tries to tell us what the *explained* event is on his view. Sometimes he says it is Brutus's thought that Caesar's constitutional policy was wrong; sometimes he says it is the stabbing itself; and at still other times it is something that Collingwood says has two sides: an *inside* which is a thought and an *outside* which is a stabbing. If this unity or combination of the outside and inside of an event[7] is what is explained by historians, we may ask what the relation is between Brutus's inside thought that Caesar's constitutional policy was wrong and the Collingwoodian combination of that inside thought and Brutus's outside blood-spilling.

Suppose we express such a Collingwoodian explanation by means of the following strange sentence in which Brutus's thought is the explainer, so to speak, and the conjunction of Brutus's thought and his action is what is explained: "Since Brutus thought Caesar's constitutional policy was wrong, Brutus thought Caesar's constitutional policy was wrong *and* Brutus spilled Caesar's blood." Here the antecedent, the statement of the explainer, is "inside" the consequent

---

[6] R. G. Collingwood, *The Idea of History* (Oxford, 1948), p. 215.
[7] Ibid., p. 213.

because it is a logical conjunct of the latter. But if we apply the logical principle that "Since p, then p and q" is equivalent to "Since p, then q" to our "since"-statement, we see that it is equivalent to the sensible statement "Since Brutus thought Caesar's constitutional policy was wrong, Brutus spilled Caesar's blood," where the antecedent statement about Brutus's thought is no longer inside the consequent statement of effect. We therefore find ourselves making a straightforward statement asserting a causal connection between an "inside" thought or belief and an "outside" action, a statement that I think may be interpreted in accordance with the regularity theory of causal explanation. Moreover, even though Brutus went through a moral argument supporting his thought or belief that Caesar's policy was wrong, the connection between the conclusion of that argument and his killing Caesar is causal. The fact that Brutus arrived at his conclusion about the wrongness of Caesar's policy by moral reasoning does not militate against viewing the connection between his concluding belief and his action in this way. A belief or thought may explain an action, and we may show that it does by appealing to a general statement about Brutus which says that whenever he is in a certain state and in certain circumstances, and believes that an action is wrong, he acts in a certain way.

Turning from Collingwood's criticism of the regularity theory, I now want to consider another objection to using it when analyzing the explanation of an event like that of Holland's prosperity—an objection made by philosophers who think that historians do not appeal to regularities. Suppose we support an explanation of Holland's rise to prosperity by appealing to a general statement like "Whenever a nation is subjected to the challenge of the sea, has excellent soil, is assisted by its neighbors in the building of dykes, and has excellent harbors, it prospers," but suppose as well that we can cite no example confirming this law except Holland at one period of its history. Can we in that case defend our singular causal statement that Holland prospered because it was challenged by the sea, had excellent soil, was assisted by its neighbors, and had an excellent maritime situation by appealing to a law for which we can produce only one confirming example?

This challenge to the regularity theory may also be illustrated by considering a generalization that Hume once asserted and could have used in an explanation. In illustrating his belief that there are principles of human nature, he once said: "Were a man whom I know to be honest and opulent, and with whom I lived in intimate friendship, to come into my house, where I am surrounded with my servants, I rest assured that he is not to stab me before he leaves in order to rob me of my silver standish."[8] Hume might have cited a related generalization when trying to defend the singular causal statement that Adam Smith did *not* on a certain occasion stab him in order to rob him of his silver standish. Let us imagine that Hume tries to explain to the police why Smith was not that person by asserting his generalization and adding the premise that Smith was an honest, opulent, intimate friend of his who came into his house while he was surrounded by his servants. Let us now imagine that Hume, when asked to support his explanation, can cite only the pair consisting of Adam Smith and himself as a confirmatory example of his generalization. This sort of situation is not peculiar to explanations dealing with human affairs. A chemist might say that a certain match lit because it was dry and was struck in a room full of oxygen, and yet be able to cite only that match when asked to supply evidence for the generalization "Whenever we strike a dry match in a room full of oxygen, it lights." Indeed, the inventor of the match might have been in that situation just after having gotten the first one to light. Does this show that the regularity theory fails to analyze the singular causal statement in this case? I do not think so, for even though the chemist's law or true universal statement *happens* to apply to a single match, it implies that every match struck in the same circumstances will light. Suppose, then, that the inventor of

---

[8] David Hume, *An Inquiry Concerning Human Understanding*, ed. Charles W. Hendel (Indianapolis, 1955), sec. VIII, part I (p. 100). This statement occurs in a paragraph that appears only in the last corrected edition of 1777, sometimes referred to as "Edition O".

the first match says just after it lights: "Whenever we strike a dry match in a room full of oxygen, it lights," and he can cite only the one match he has lit. In spite of that, the inventor implies—if he thinks he has asserted a law—that a second match will also obey the law. Something similar may be true of Hume's generalization. It is a contingent truth that the subject-term of a generalization happens to apply to only one example, since the critic of the regularity theory cannot prove that as we complicate the subject-term of the chemist's generalization—"dry match struck in a room full of oxygen"—we *must*, in order to arrive at a true generalization, state one which applies to only one example. Even if Holland happened at one time to be the only nation that responded to the challenge of the sea while it had the advantages of a good soil, an excellent maritime situation, and expertise at dyke building, other such nations might have existed in the past and might appear in the future.

Let us suppose, however, that in fact there is no other past or future confirmatory example. What then? Then the explanation is shaky *if* its advocate can present no further evidence in its behalf (such as a more general theory that logically implies the generalization), and the regularity theory has the virtue of bringing out the shakiness of such an explanation. Can we seriously maintain that Geyl's explanation of the rise of Holland would be acceptable if (1) *no* other nation has behaved, does behave, or will behave as Holland did in those circumstances; (2) we have no knowledge of a theory that will imply Geyl's assumed generalization; and (3) we have no way of creating another confirming instance artificially? I doubt it. Often, of course, when an explanation whose generalization applies to only one example is presented, there are other ways of supporting the generalization. If the inventor of the match should say, just after he has succeeded in getting the first match to light, that it lit because it was dry and struck in the presence of a lot of oxygen, he might defend his generalization about matches by deducing it from chemical laws concerning the behavior of sulfur and the statement that matches are made of sulfur. And Hume, in defense of the generalization mentioned earlier, might have pointed out that honest men usually do not rob, that opulent men usually do not rob, that friends of long standing usually do not stab one in the presence of one's servants; and he might have added that all these truths together supply strong evidence for the generalization that no opulent, honest friend of long standing would ever stab one in the presence of one's servants in order to rob one. He might have said that since each one of these truths contributes to the plausibility of his generalization, together they make it almost certain—especially if he were to add that the putative robber is sane.

Let us suppose now that Geyl formulates his multifactored, complicated explanation of the rise of Holland in a deductive argument whose generalization applies to only one example without deducing his generalization from other truths, and that he cites no other nation in support of his generalization. In that case, Geyl's explanation would be in trouble. It would be inadequately supported, an inadequacy revealed by our having formulated it in the terms advocated by the regularist. One might ask, of course, whether every complicated historical explanation must suffer the same fate, but I see no reason to believe so. The historian may find himself in this predicament more often than the natural scientist does, but this merely shows what we all know—that historical causal explanations are, generally speaking, less reliable and more difficult to defend than those presented in natural science. So far, then, from being unfaithful to the thought and language of history, the regularity theory of explanation may be said to reveal one of historical language's characteristic features. Historical explanations are generally more debatable, more subject to doubt than the explanations of natural scientists, in part because they *are* often based on complex generalizations that apply only to single instances and that are *not* supported in other ways—a defect that the regularity or covering law theory reveals. That theory also helps us see the limitations of the speculative philosophies of history that Hegel, Vico, Comte, and Marx had proposed, and helps explain why they became suspect when philosophers called attention to their reliance on obscure entities like Hegel's World Spirit, on Vico's various natures of man, and on the dubious belief of Marx's collaborator Friedrich Engels that the laws of history can be deduced from a metaphysical theory such as dialectical materialism. Unfortunately, however, disenchantment with the speculative philosophy of history has led some philosophical critics of the regularity theory to reject *any* appeal to regularity as a logical component of explanation—to throw out the baby of Hume's regularity theory with the bathwater of his speculation.

The tendency to throw both of them out together was in part encouraged by the tendency of regularists such as Hume to appeal to *debatable* laws of human nature by contrast to the one of his that I mentioned earlier. It was Hume who wrote that a historian who wants to know the sentiments, inclinations, and course of life of the Greeks and Romans would do well to study well the temper and actions of the French and English because "you cannot be much mistaken" in applying to the earlier two nations most of the observations made about the two later ones. "Mankind are so much the same, in all times and places," Hume observed, "that history informs us of nothing new or strange in this particular. Its chief use is only to discover the constant and universal principles of human nature by showing men in all varieties of circumstances and situations, and furnishing us with materials from which we may form our observations and become acquainted with the regular springs of human action and behavior."[9] But we must bear in mind that Hume defended two distinct doctrines—the plausible regularity or covering law theory of causation, as well as the debatable theory that there are transcultural regularities in human nature—and that valid arguments against the second theory do not reflect adversely on the first; for Hume, like most philosophers, was probably better at analyzing historical explanations than he was at giving them.

[9] Ibid., p. 93.

Explanation and Interest

Having examined the view that a historical explanation of an event or condition may be supported by appealing to true general statements and to what have been called true statements of initial conditions, I shall now consider the role of the historian's interest when he presents a historical explanation. We have seen that the challenge of the sea may be a contributory or partial cause of Holland's rise and that another contributory or partial cause of Holland's rise might also be singled out in a singular "because"-statement. For example, one historian might say that Holland became prosperous because it had excellent ports, while another might say that it became prosperous because it was challenged by the sea. These two historians may both be speaking truthfully because they approach the event from different points of view that correspond to their different interests. To say how and why, we should observe first that we normally try to explain events that are unusual, such as accidents, catastrophes, or wars; and if an event is unusual, we may seek its unusual causal antecedent.

Thus, if Adam has an attack of indigestion, his wife Eve and his physician may present different causal explanations of that event.[10] Eve, though she knows that Adam has ulcers, may say that he had his attack because he ate an apple at lunch. His apple eating may be called the *chief contributing cause for Eve*, even though she knows that Adam's having ulcers combined with his eating of the apple to form what Mill calls the whole cause. A physician, on the other hand, who knows that Adam has eaten an apple may say that the chief contributing cause of Adam's indigestion was the ulcerated condition of Adam's stomach, since the physician thinks that that is what makes Adam an abnormal patient. By contrast, John Stuart Mill

---

[10] For this example and much illumination on the subject of causation, see H. L. A. Hart and A. M. Honoré, *Causation in the Law* (Oxford, 1959), pp. 33–34.

sometimes says that both of them speak falsely because he thinks that *the* cause, which he calls the whole cause,[11] is a combination of what Eve calls *the* cause and what the doctor calls *the* cause from their different points of view. However, since Eve and the doctor may know that two things cooperated to bring about Adam's indigestion, they may acknowledge that when they speak of *the* cause, they are speaking elliptically. In that case Eve's statement would be expanded into "The cause of Adam's attack *from my point of view* is his having eaten an apple," whereas the doctor's statement would be expanded into "The cause of Adam's attack *from my point of view* is the ulcerated condition of his stomach." The wife's point of view is that of someone who asks: "Why did Adam, who doesn't always have indigestion, have it today?" Her answer to the question is "Because he ate an apple at lunch," since eating an apple was the factor that from her point of view explains Adam's departure from his normal state. And what is the physician's standpoint? It is that of someone who asks, "Why did Adam have an attack of indigestion when not all of my patients who eat apples have such an attack?" and who answers, "Because Adam has ulcers." For the physician, having ulcers makes the difference—it is the condition that explains why Adam had an attack of indigestion; whereas the event of eating an apple is what makes the difference for Eve. Therefore, we see that they are answering different questions and so both can be speaking truthfully, much as two observers who look at a penny from different angles do not contradict each other when one says that it looks circular to her whereas the other says that it looks elliptical to him.

Let us now return to historical explanation, which exhibits a similar variation in the answers to "why?"-questions when they are expanded with the questioner's standpoint or interest in mind. Some historians resemble Eve when they ask such questions, while some resemble the physician. A historian who resembles Eve is an event

---

[11] J. S. Mill, *System of Logic, Ratiocinative and Inductive: Being a Connected View of the Principles of Evidence, and the Methods of Scientific Investigation*, ed. J. M. Robson (Toronto, 1973), book III, chap. 5, sec. 3 (1:332).

seeker who says that the cause, or the main cause, of the First World War was the assassination of the archduke of Austria at Sarajevo, whereas the historian who resembles the physician says that its main cause was a combination of so-called underlying factors such as commercial rivalries, alliances of nations, and territorial ambitions. While some historians seem to think that underlying causes or states are "truer" causes or more real contributory causes, the eminent historian Henri Pirenne identified an *event*, the Muslim invasion of the seventh and eighth centuries, as the cause of the collapse of what he calls the Mediterranean Commonwealth,[12] and I daresay that other historians have said similar things. Pirenne held that this event explained the disruption of social, political, and cultural conditions that had survived the invasion of the barbarians from the north. Of course, the Muslim invasion took longer than Adam's eating of an apple, but the invasion was nevertheless an *event* rather than a state. That is why one historian's answer to the question "Why did the First World War occur?" may refer to an event—the assassination of the archduke—if the historian frames her question in the manner of Eve, but another answer may be given by another historian who frames his question in the manner of the physician.

It follows that the construction of a narrative depends in part on which contributory factors a historian focuses when asserting different singular causal statements. We should note, furthermore, that it is rare to find a history that cites only states as causes or only events as causes. The biographer, for example, may begin by saying that a certain event brought about a certain state and then go on to say that that state explained a later event. The event of firing on Fort Sumter might be said by an American historian to have brought about the state of war between the North and South, and that state of war might then be cited to explain the event of one army attacking another at a later time. In a brief history of a royal family, we may say that the king's death (event) caused the queen to be anxious

---

[12] Henri Pirenne, *Medieval Cities: Their Origins and the Revival of Trade*, trans. Frank D. Halsey (Princeton, 1939), pp. 24–25.

(state); the queen's anxiety caused her to flee the kingdom (event); the queen's flight led the prince to be depressed (state); the prince's depression led him to commit suicide (event); the prince's suicide led to the loneliness of the princess (state); and her loneliness led her to remarry (event). Thus a narrative historian may oscillate between speaking causally in the manner of Eve and speaking causally in the manner of Adam's physician. It is her *interest* that leads one historian to select an event as the main contributory cause of an event in the manner of Eve, and it is a different *interest* that leads another historian to select a state as the contributory cause of that event in the manner of the physician. Moreover, there seems to be no Archimedean point, as it were, from which we can survey such interests and declare one to be superior to another; it is hard to defend the view that one interest is correct for a historian to have whereas the other is not.

Let us now turn our attention from an isolated causal statement to a conjunction of causal statements that constitutes a narrative as opposed to a chronicle of the United States of America, where a chronicle lists in temporal order statements about events and states without asserting causal connections between them. A historian's chronicle—by contrast to a historian's narrative—will list certain events or states as central or major: for example, the Revolution, the Civil War, the First World War, the Great Depression, the Second World War, and the cold war. It is the historian's interest that determines his selection of these items. They are entrenched items that will be included in all or most chronicles of the United States at a given time because a historian's interest in them is dictated in part by what James called the principle of conservatism: he includes them because other historians have included them. That is also why some items included at one time may be omitted in the future; for example, statements recording the occurrence of the Mexican War and the Spanish-American War may disappear from a chronicle of the United States because historians cease to be interested in them. In other words, one reason why history is rewritten is that some entrenched events cease to be entrenched. Once the entrenched items are fixed, the narrative historian will begin with the first one, and then fill the gaps between others by interpolating other items. Such interpolation will be governed by an Eve-like or a doctor-like interest in contributory causes, as well as by an interest-determined choice of entrenched items that fixes the *terminus a quo* and the *terminus ad quem* of the story.

Consequently, because the historian's interest *and* his desire to speak truthfully both play a part in the construction of a narrative, the historical critic who reads the first historian's narrative may not only ask whether his singular causal statements are true but also whether all of the historian's entrenched items should remain entrenched, and whether the interpolated items are determined by adopting a viewpoint that the critic shares. A historical critic who has an interest like Eve's will approve of an Eve-like causal statement, whereas a critic whose interest is like that of the doctor will approve of a doctor-like causal statement. But, as I have said, it is difficult to show objectively that one of these points of view is in general superior to others, which seems to indicate that there are no obvious rules of historical practice that dictate one such selection rather than another. This situation is not unlike the art critic's on Dewey's view, and for that reason there is an element of art in the historian's enterprise.

The role of interest in historical study also has counterparts in the holistic pragmatist's view of scientific theorizing. One is the tendency of historians to retain statements in their chronicle that their predecessors have entrenched, much as the physicist cleaves to the principle of conservation of energy and statements of mathematics and logic unless she has very good reason to abandon them. But this conservatism does not preclude the jettisoning of certain entrenched items, as we have seen. A second counterpart is the tendency of the historian to explain items that he regards as important, a tendency that corresponds to the physicist's desire to explain data that *she* regards as important. And a third is the historian's tendency to organize his data simply or elegantly. These are all tendencies to rely on what James regarded as the virtues of a scientific theory; they correspond to the pragmatic considerations to which the scientist appeals when organizing experiences or data. A physicist regards a good theory as a *simple* or *elegant* explanation of important data that is not too disruptive of older ways of thinking; and a historian regards a good narrative analogously. Furthermore, even though a narrative does not contain general truths, each causal statement in a story may rely on an unstated general truth; for example, one causal statement above about our royal family relies on a psychological generalization supporting the claim that the king's death caused the queen, who was of a certain temperament, to flee. Such reliance on a generalization shows that historical thinking is holistic, since a historian who is asked why he accepts a singular causal statement may often be coaxed into presenting the generalization on which he had relied as well as the singular statements which join with that generalization in implying the statement that reports what he explained. Failing that, the historian may try to present his reasons for believing that there *is* such a conjunction. But if he fails to do even that, we may doubt that he has explained what he says he has explained.

Narration and Interest

Once we accept that a historian's singular causal statement depends on the viewpoint from which he selects one contributory cause rather than another, and once we accept that his interest may determine his *terminus a quo* and his *terminus ad quem* as well as other states or events that he regards as entrenched milestones in the chronicle of his subject, we see that neither his history nor his chronicle may be called a map, a copy, a picture, or a mirror of some antecedent reality. A chronicle of a nation is the result of removing causal words from its history, and therefore consists of the noncausal singular statements that serve as the antecedents or the consequents of singular causal statements in a history. The historian says that a nation's being at war caused an enemy fort to be fired on, whereas the chronicler merely says "The nation was at war" and "The enemy fort was fired on." As E. M. Forster remarks somewhere, a chronicler leads a reader who has heard the first sentence to ask "And then what?" whereas a historian will ask "So what?" The historian wants to know what happened as a causal consequence of what the chronicle recorded in the first sentence. But since one true history of a nation may contain causal statements that differ from those in another equally true history of it, and since each history implies a chronicle, there are as many different (and possibly overlapping) true chronicles of a nation as there are different true histories of that nation. Although a chronicle is implied by a history, this does not mean that Taine was right in declaring that the historian first chronicles his facts and then seeks the causal relations between them. Even though a history logically implies its associated chronicle whereas the chronicle does not logically imply the history, in constructing a chronicle and in constructing a history the historian oscillates between one activity and the other. He may alter his narrative because he has changed his chronicle, and he may alter his chronicle because he has changed his narrative.

It may therefore help to think of a historian's task in more simple cases as that of drawing a causal line segment between items in a particular chronicle: these are points on a plane that represents all the items in the career of a nation like the United States of America. Let us suppose that a historian decides to begin with the Revolution as his initial item and also to include other entrenched items. In that case he may draw a line segment that runs through all his selected points from the Revolution to, let us say, the end of the cold war. The line segment he draws may represent his history, whereas unconnected points—items—make up his chronicle. Because reality does not, so to speak, force the historian to include the singular noncausal statements included in his chronicle, and because it does not force him to include the singular causal statements included in that history, the narrative line segment he produces is not one that reality forces him to produce. Because other historians may select other termini and other intervening points, they will draw different line segments, though different historical line segments may intersect at various places; and they may also share linear subsegments. I want to stress, however, that a history and a chronicle of an entity are conjunctions of *truths* about an entity such as a nation, and that the truth of the conjoined statements does not depend on the interests of the historian; his interests do not determine that Washington crossed the Delaware but they do determine whether he includes that statement in his chronicle. Relativity or subjectivity enters the picture when the historian decides *what truths* to assert as opposed to those that he omits.

Concentrating on the role of interest in the formation of a chronicle, I want to consider certain views of it that I think are misleading. These views do not deal directly with chronicles but they bear on the problem of selection, as we shall see. In one of his essays on London, Henry James said that he was presenting a "genial summary" about that city. Because London was immense, he said, he could not speak of it as a whole. It was a collection of wholes, and so he asked, "Of which them is it more important to speak?" Inevitably, he said, "there must be a choice, and I know of none more scientific than simply to leave out what we may have to apologize for. The uglinesses, the 'rookeries,' the brutalities, the night-aspect of many of the streets, and the hour when they are cleared out before closing—there are many elements of this kind which have to be counted out before a genial summary can be made."[13] This so-called scientific criterion resembled that proffered by James's contemporary William Dean Howells, who sometimes focused in his novels on what he called "the smiling aspects of life."

---

[13] Henry James, *Essays in London and Elsewhere* (New York, 1893), p. 27.

If James and Howells were historians who used such criteria, they would have selected a chronicle on the basis of their esthetic or moral evaluation of points in the plane I have mentioned; and Samuel Eliot Morison, the American historian, once adopted a closely related view of history. He tells us that in his youth he thought that a historian of the United States should adopt a Federalist–Whig–Republican standpoint and take a dim view of all Democratic leaders except Grover Cleveland. But by the middle of the twentieth century, Morison continued, it was difficult to find a good history of the country that did not follow the "Jefferson–Jackson–Franklin D. Roosevelt line." He himself was converted to the second line, according to Morison, when he discovered in his first researches on New England Federalism that "the 'wise and good and rich' whom Fisher Ames thought should rule the nation were stupid, narrow-minded, and local in outlook."[14] It seems, therefore, that Morison was guided in the construction of his history and of his chronicle by his evaluation of the leaders he studied, and we may regard his conversion and attendant shift from one chronicle to another as based on a reevaluation of those leaders. However, a chronicle based only on a historian's evaluation of leaders is not likely to have its components connected in a history in which those components are linked by causal connections. A narrative historian interested in the *development* of his subject who begins his chronicle with a congenial item will often find that it has effects that are not congenial; items toward which he is favorably disposed may, like people, have unattractive antecedents and unattractive offspring.

Reacting against the view that a chronicle of a nation records only events or states toward which the historian is favorably disposed, some writers have maintained that the historian and the chronicler should present the supposedly objective essence or spirit of the central subject. According to Aristotle, history is different from philoso-

---

[14] Samuel Eliot Morison, *By Land and By Sea: Essays and Addresses* (New York, 1953), pp. 356–57.

phy because history cannot discern the essence of the human species or of an individual such as Socrates, but some historians seem to think that they can report items that *are* essential to the individual. Take, for example, the following remark by a well-known historian in a review of the biography of a scientist: "Facts are facts. But there are other facts too. When all is set down, the real character—that elusive, burning character whose flame formed the thick crust around it—becomes clear. Behind the anti-Semitic utterances we see tireless, successful efforts to rescue Jewish scientists from Germany. Behind the sneers at the 'humanities' we see the positive desire to widen both scientific and humane education. Behind the withdrawn, personal austerity, we see the real belief that others should have a full life, and a proper material basis for it, even in war. We also see what his real wartime services were."[15] One wonders why the author of this passage did not add that beneath his hero's harsh exterior there beat a heart of gold!

This historian's appeal to the essence of an individual is reminiscent of that made by an earnest character in Dostoyevsky's *The Possessed* who claims that her historical work will present "the spiritual, moral, inner life of Russia for a whole year";[16] and it is reminiscent of the Hegelian idea that the historian seeks the essential spirit of an age. However, the doctrine that individuals have essences was challenged by Locke and by John Stuart Mill, and William James tried to pragmatize it, so to speak. He declared that "all ways of conceiving a concrete fact, if they are true ways at all, are equally true ways. *There is no property* ABSOLUTELY essential to any one thing."[17] Therefore, James held, the question "What is that?"—asked as the questioner points to a concrete object—may be answered in many different true statements, depending on the practical concerns of the questioner or the respondent. The thing upon

[15] H. R. Trevor-Roper, review of the Earl of Birkenhead's *The Professor and the Prime Minister, New York Times Book Review*, February 25, 1962, p. 3.

[16] Fyodor Dostoyevsky, *The Possessed*, [trans. Constance Garnett], Everyman ed. (New York, 1931), 1:114–16.

[17] William James, *The Principles of Psychology* (New York, 1890), 2:333.

which he was writing, James said, might be regarded as a surface for inscription, or as a combustible material, or as a thin thing, or as a hydrocarbonaceous thing, or as a thing eight by ten inches in size, or as an American thing, and so on. *What* one regards it as, depends, James said, on what one wants to do with it; and since one can do only one of these things at a time, James added, one can regard it in only one of these ways at a time.

It is easy to see the implications of this view of an individual's essence for a view of the chronicle of a subject. One might say that the entire chronicle stands to a chronicler's aims as James's calling his piece of paper a combustible object stands to his aim of lighting a fire—except for the fact that a chronicle is a long conjunction of singular statements, whereas a Jamesian pragmatic statement of essence, like an Aristotelian, is conveyed in one comparatively brief declaration. According to James, when we say that one predicate is *the* predicate that answers the question "What is that?" we are speaking elliptically. When speaking nonelliptically, he claimed, we may ask: "What is the predicate of that by virtue of which I can use it as kindling, for example?" Although it is tempting to transfer this view to the case of *the* chronicle of a person or a nation, it cannot be applied to a dead and buried individual or to an extinct civilization with which the historian cannot deal overtly. A reader of a chronicle of ancient Athens might, of course, learn something that would help him change today's United States, but not every historian writes a chronicle of ancient Greece with the intention of instructing a reformer. A historian might try to construct a chronicle of ancient Greece that would be of use to a reformer of contemporary America, but, like Henry James's genial summary of London, such a chronicle would not always follow from a causally integrated history that traces the development of ancient Greece. At best such a genial chronicle would consist of disconnected statements that might supply isolated useful information to practically oriented readers.

Once we abandon various esthetic, moral, essentialist, and practically oriented views of a chronicle, we may say that a superior one—

or one that we should present in answer to the question "What truths should a chronicler assert about that?"—expresses a *fuller* or more complete truth about its subject. The chronicler, it might be said, tries to approximate the whole truth about its subject; therefore one chronicle will be judged better than another if it comes closer to the whole truth about that subject than the second does. In this vein, the historian Macaulay once wrote:

> No picture . . . and no history can present us with the whole truth; but those are the best pictures and the best histories which exhibit such parts of the truth as most nearly produce the effect of the whole. He who is deficient in the art of selection may, by showing nothing but the truth, produce all the effect of the greatest falsehood. It perpetually happens that one writer tells less truth than another, merely because he tells more truths. In the imitative arts we constantly see this. There are lines in the human face . . . which stand in such relations to each other that they ought either to be all introduced into a painting together or all omitted together. A sketch in which none of them enters may be excellent; but, if some are given and others left out, though there are more points of likeness, there is less likeness. An outline scrawled with a pen, which seizes *the marked features of a countenance* [my emphasis], will give a much stronger idea of it than a bad painting in oils. Yet the worst painting in oils . . . resembles the original in many more particulars. A bust of white marble may give an excellent idea of a blooming face. Color the lips and cheeks, leaving the hair and eyes unaltered, and the similarity, instead of being more striking, will be less so.[18]

Although I think Macaulay misleadingly suggests that a historian aims at the whole truth about a subject that cannot be attained, Macaulay is right to deny that the task of the historian is to amass more and more truths about his subject. Macaulay writes as though there were a subject that the historian and his critic can observe, and as

---

[18] Thomas Babington Macaulay, *Critical and Historical Essays* (New York, 1900), 1:244–45.

though the partial truth expressed in one chronicle comes closer than others to having the same effect as the whole truth about the subject has on both of them. But neither the historian nor his critic can know the whole truth about a subject so as to compare it with a partial truth in order to see whether the latter has the "same effect" as the former. The critic cannot watch the historian and his departed subject while the historian paints a picture of that subject; she cannot turn from the historian's canvas to his subject in order to see whether the historian is coming closer to the whole truth about the subject or veering from it. The picture or copy view of history is as inadequate, therefore, as the picture or copy view of scientific theory. We are not able to resuscitate the late Middle Ages to discover whether its "most striking feature . . . was an exceptionally strong sense of guilt and a truly dreadful fear of attribution, seeking expression in a passionate longing for effective intercession and in a craving for direct, personal experience of the Deity, as well as in a corresponding dissatisfaction with the Church and with the mechanization of the means of salvation."[19] Even if—*per impossibile*—we were to resuscitate an extinct item of the past, not all historical observers of it would converge on one feature of it as "most striking"—the counterpart of Macaulay's "marked features of a countenance." The reference to the marked or most striking feature of the late Middle Ages is in some ways like the reference to a unique essence or spirit. The most striking is not said to be the deepest feature—as the essence is supposed to be—but the most conspicuous one. Even if we could revive a bygone society, there might be disagreement about which of its features was the most conspicuous, simply because conspicuousness may vary from one historian to another according to the viewpoint of each.

Just as the picture theory of theoretical statements in physics has been abandoned in the philosophy of natural science, so the picture theory of a history or of a chronicle should be abandoned in the

---

[19] William L. Langer, "The Next Assignment," *American Historical Review* 63 (1958): 298.

philosophy of history. History is not an imitative art, so it does not help to say that historians seek the essence or spirit of the historical subject if they cannot compare what they write with that dubious entity; it does not help to say that they try to approximate the whole truth if they cannot know what the whole truth is and if, as Macaulay claims, merely amassing more truths does not get us closer to the whole truth; it does not help to say that the historian tries to produce a partial truth whose effect most nearly produces the unknowable effect of the whole truth. What, then, shall we say? It seems to me that we should recognize that the interests of the historian determine (a) his *terminus a quo* and his *terminus ad quem*, (b) the entrenched and the major intervening items in his chronicle, and (c) the items he selects as causes from his varying points of view. In that case, we should also recognize that his construction of a history is determined not only by the historian's interest in telling nothing but the truth but also by his other interests. Therefore when a historical critic approves of a history as a whole, the critic not only expresses her agreement with the historian's causal statements but she indicates that the historian's selection of items in his chronicle meets with her approval. In other words, the critic agrees with the historian about the facts; she shares the historian's point of view, and therefore his interests; and she believes that the historian's chronicle is the one that she would herself present.

I should add that I am speaking of what is called a general history of a subject like a society, for one expects a specialized historian to concentrate on one aspect of the nation—to approach it, for example, from an economic or a political point of view. By adopting such an approach the historian might hope to create a chronicle that contains only singular economic or political truths causally linked in a history; but even here it may be argued that some singular economic truths in a chronicle of a society cannot be explained by citing *only* other economic truths and by assuming only economic laws. And an analogous argument may be made even more plausibly in the case of a purely political history. But one of the important achievements of nineteenth-century historical thought was to recognize with Vico, Hegel, and Marx the value of writing general history with eyes trained on the interconnections of political, legal, economic, and ideological truths about a society. Of course, another view of the nineteenth century was that one sort of truth—for example, economic truth—was in some sense fundamental, that by knowing only economic truths about a society, one could predict and explain *all* of the other truths about it or, in a weaker version of this view, that the economic factor in history was the most important one. But such a monistic approach to general history suffers from a failure to clarify the notion of an important factor, and that is why most general histories of a society or nation tend to be pluralistic, meaning that the contributory causes that historians select are not all economic, political, or intellectual and that the same is true of their chronicles. The idea that historians report *only* congenial truths, or only essential truths, or only practical truths, or only economic truths about their central subject is as deficient as the view that they try to present something that approximates that obscure entity, the whole truth about that subject.

Accepting this sort of pluralism permits us to see why different historians may present different true histories of one nation, but it also may lead us to ask another question: Does the view that all historians select the true statements they make in their chronicles on the basis of their interests license the selections made by politically or religiously tendentious historians and the distortion that they sometimes engage in? Can the view of history I have been defending be used to justify such distortion? I think not. Suppose some Soviet historian had said that he approached the history of his nation with a point of view from which he could justifiably erase the role of Leon Trotsky as a leader of the Russian Revolution. Such a historian might have said during the heyday of the Soviet Union that Trotsky was an enemy of the working class, and that his views and actions were so repugnant to the aims of the Soviet Union that everything possible should be done by historians to avoid enhancing his reputation. In keeping with such a political interest, this historian might have claimed to be justified in playing down Trotsky's role in the October Revolution, even to the point of writing that he played no role at all in it. In that case, of course, the Soviet historian would be making a false statement, which obviously runs counter to my view that nothing but the truth should appear in a chronicle. But another method of distortion would consist in *ignoring* Trotsky's role by saying nothing about him in one's history of the Russian Revolution. In that case one would not make a false statement, and one would not violate the principle that one should tell nothing but the truth. Indeed, an advocate of telling *the whole truth* might reenter the debate by saying that our tendentious Soviet historian erred precisely because he did not tell the whole truth, that his distortion consisted in ignoring a truth. So now we are brought back to the question: "Is there a whole truth about the Russian Revolution that a historian *should* tell and that he fails to tell when he omits Trotsky's role in it?" Need we say, in order to dissociate ourselves from the dishonest and politically tendentious approach of the selective Soviet historian, that every historian should come as close as possible to this whole truth? Let us keep in mind, while trying to answer this question, that the Soviet historian says that he has an interest in not including the truth about Trotsky in his history, thereby acting in line with the view that historians construct their chronicles in accordance with their interests. How can we consistently condemn the Soviet historian while defending the position that all historians engage in selection determined by their interests and yet refusing to say that historians should approximate the whole truth about their subject?

I think we may answer by saying that ignoring Trotsky's role in the Russian Revolution would be like ignoring laboratory data that would count against a theory in natural science, thereby saving the theory and gaining the dishonest scientist a promotion. An interest in getting a promotion might be used to justify such fraud just as an interest in not enhancing Trotsky's reputation might be said to justify disregarding his role in the October Revolution, and as an interest in winning a chess game might be said to justify removing the opponent's queen while he was not looking at the board. This is not to say that scientists never suppress data, that chess players never commit fraud, or that poker players never use marked cards. But it is to say that there are rules that historians, like scientists, generally observe—and one of them is that a practical political interest should not dictate ignoring a truth. However, there is no rule that prohibits acting on an interest such as Eve's in selecting an event as the cause of an event, and there is no rule that prohibits acting on an interest like that of the doctor in selecting a state as the cause. Such an acceptable form of selecting what truth to include or exclude is not guided by an objectionable interest, whereas the interest that motivates our Soviet historian is objectionable by the standards accepted by most historians.

With this in mind, we should observe the difference between two pairs of historians. One pair consists of a historian A, who says that the assassination of the archduke at Sarajevo was the cause of the First World War, and of another historian B, who says instead that a combination of entangling alliances, commercial rivalries, and territorial ambitions was the cause. A second pair consists of a historian C, who says that Lenin and Trotsky led the Russian Revolution, and of another historian D, who merely says that Lenin led the Russian Revolution. Both A and B may be speaking truthfully, since they answer different questions in the manner of Eve and the physician. But C and D oppose each other in a different way: D is motivated by a desire to diminish the role of Trotsky because he thinks Trotsky became an enemy of the Revolution, whereas C is not so motivated. D's interest is based on political prejudice and is therefore prohibited by the rules of the historical game, much as an interest in winning does not support removing the queen of one's opponent in chess while he is not looking. Notice that D does not say that Trotsky was *not* a leader of the revolution; he merely ignores Trotsky because he does not want to be accused of outright lying. He tries to keep his reader in ignorance of Trotsky's role and thereby accomplishes his politically tendentious goal without telling a blatant lie. Nevertheless he is motivated by an objectionable interest in withholding a truth. Notice also that the rule of history that says that historians should not behave as D does is a prohibition, just as most rules of morality are. It is in the same class as "Don't use marked cards in poker," "Don't remove your opponent's queen in chess when he isn't looking," or "Don't blow cigar smoke at your opponent in chess in order to unsettle her." These do not appear in rule books of poker or chess, just as the corresponding rules of history do not appear in any written set of rules about historical writing. But they are generally accepted by those who call themselves historians—at least in our culture—and they help us distinguish the acceptable difference of interest exhibited by A and B from that exhibited by C and D.

Therefore, when I say that a historian selects the items in his chronicle on the basis of his interest, I refer to an interest that does not violate ethical rules of the historical game. An interest that impels a politically or religiously motivated selector of items in a chronicle is an interest that is condemned in the light of moral rules such as those that forbid lying or cheating in general, whereas an interest in selecting an event rather than a state or vice versa as the principal contributory cause of an event or state is not condemned by moral rules. For this reason A and B are not likely to call each other liars or cheats, whereas C may call D a liar when lying is construed broadly enough to include withholding a known truth, and D may call C an enemy of the working class.

This has been a relatively long chapter for several reasons, one of them connected with my special interest in the philosophy of history, and another with my desire to show by example how far twentieth-century philosophers of history came from speculative theorizing about the past. Later philosophers did not appeal to the doings of Hegel's Absolute Mind or derive theories by deduction from a

rationalistic metaphysics. Instead they studied the role of generalization and interest in explanation and narration, thereby showing
their kinship with philosophers such as Duhem, who studied the
behavior of physicists; with philosophers such as James, who studied
the varieties of religious experience; and with philosophers such as
Dewey, who examined the creative processes of artists. Other post-
rationalistic philosophers who moved in this direction also contrib-
uted to the renewal of an intelligible philosophy of culture, as we
shall see when we examine the work of Nelson Goodman on art and
John Rawls on political morality. Their work shows how philosophers in the analytic and linguistic tradition who outgrew the remnants of classical rationalism provided a powerful alternative to the
maunderings of obscurantists who claim to be the custodians of culture in our time.

VIII

Philosophy of Art as Philosophy of Language

Nelson Goodman

A T THE BEGINNING OF THE TWENTIETH CEN-
tury, American philosophers such as James,
Royce, Santayana, and Dewey wrote about religion, science, art, education, history, and politics; but as the century wore on, younger
philosophers focused more narrowly on natural science, on logic,
and on ordinary language under the influence of Carnap's view that
philosophy is neither more nor less than the logical analysis of science or of G. E. Moore's view that a major task of philosophy is to
clarify the meanings of ordinary words such as "see," "true," and
"good." Thus Moore once dismissed Santayana's study *The Life of
Reason* (1905–06)—a five-volume work in the philosophy of culture
that dealt with art, religion, morals, and science—by saying, "This
book is so wanting in clearness of thought that I doubt whether it
can be of much use to anyone."[1] One effect of this preoccupation
with clarity was a tendency to shy away from analyzing statements
of politics, of history, of religion, and of art, perhaps because they
were thought to be too obscure to be fit subjects for clarification—
not clear enough to be made clearer, as it were. Partly for this reason,

[1] G. E. Moore, *International Journal of Ethics* 17 (1906–07): 248.

philosophical analysts focused on mathematics, on natural science, and on commonsense statements, thinking they could be sure that 5 is a number and that they often saw rabbits, tables, and chairs.

One task of philosophical analysts therefore became that of analyzing the concept of number in the manner of Frege and Russell, and that of perception by saying that "Moore sees a rabbit" means the same as "There is something that Moore sees directly which is a considerable part of the surface of a rabbit." Such an analysis might also read: "The proposition that Moore sees a rabbit is identical with the proposition that there is something that Moore sees directly which is a considerable part of the surface of a rabbit," where a proposition was conceived as an abstract extralinguistic entity. Having presented such an analysis, some philosophers focused on what it was that Moore saw *directly* and asked: Is it physical, as the rabbit is, or is it not physical? And if it is not physical, what is it? At this point a nonphysical entity called a sense-datum was often introduced into the discussion as the intermediate entity, and it was said to be something like an afterimage. Some analysts thought that in addition to rabbits, which were denoted by the word "rabbit", there exists the attribute of being a rabbit, which was regarded as the meaning or connotation of "rabbit"; and they also held that a philosopher should recognize the existence of yet another entity, the extralinguistic proposition that is expressed by the sentence "Moore sees a rabbit." The proposition was said to be *the meaning* of a sentence, and it figured centrally in the attack that Moore and Russell leveled against James's pragmatic theory of truth. James responded to their criticism by saying that his theory of truth was not an effort to analyze a shadowy proposition that hovers between a sentence and the world, and other philosophers objected to Moore's interposing a sense-datum between himself and the rabbit as well as an attribute between an adjective and a class.

In an ironic development, philosophers who refused to analyze statements in religion, politics, law, and history because they found them too unclear to be analyzed asserted the existence of philosoph-

ical entities such as attributes, propositions, and sense-data in statements that were thought by their critics to be even less clear. This
difficulty was compounded by Moore's admission that his notion of
analysis rested on an unclear notion of analytic statement, an admission that converged at midcentury with the doubts of Goodman,
Quine, and others that any clear criterion of analyticity could be
provided. Along with such doubts went the view that if and when
analyticity were ever provided with a usable criterion, it would turn
out to be a matter of degree, so that we could say that some sentences were more or less analytic than others. Running through
these discussions was the view that the concept of synonymy that
underlay analyticity and the concept of analyticity itself were empirical, that we can tell only by empirical investigation of language that
a sentence like "Socrates is a man" is synonymous with "Socrates is
a rational animal" but not with "Socrates has opposable thumbs."
The idea that synonymy and analyticity are established empirically
went along with the view that much of philosophy is empirical and
the belief that one should breach the epistemic wall that was thought
to exist between the *a priori* philosophical analysis of scientific and
commonsense statements and *a posteriori* investigations of art such
as Dewey carried on in *Art as Experience*.

Goodman on Likeness of Meaning

In the work of Nelson Goodman on art, especially his *Languages of
Art* (1968), we find a subtle way of linking the philosophy of art and
the philosophy of science so as to avoid speaking about entities that
other philosophers talked about quite freely. Indeed, he not only
declined to analyze propositions conceived as the meaning of sentences, he declined to say that linguistic expressions are synonymous
in the sense favored by some analytic philosophers. His skepticism
about synonymy was partly responsible for his abandoning the traditional analytic question "What is art?" in favor of "When is art?"—

thereby following a path that resembled the one James took when he tried to shake off critics of his theory of truth. Just as James maintained that he did not seek a synonym of "true", Goodman denied that he sought a synonym of "artistic"; indeed, after abandoning a search for synonyms, he adopted a semantic theory that led him to say that no two distinct expression are synonymous. His refusal to ask "What is art?" reflected his refusal to search for a Platonic attribute that is identical with being artistic or for a synonym of "artistic". Instead he sought what he called the symptoms of art, and his search for them rather than for the essence of art or the meaning of "art" was indicative of his desire to take an empirical approach to the philosophy of art that resembled Dewey's in many respects, as we shall see.

With Quine and myself, Goodman rejected the view that two predicates such as "man" and "rational animal" are synonymous because they express or connote the same Platonic concept or attribute; but Goodman went further and said that calling them synonymous was so obscure that he did not know what philosophers who sought a behavioristic criterion for synonymy were seeking.[2] He therefore refused to say that "Every man is a rational animal" is analytic whereas "Every man is a featherless biped" is synthetic, insisting that the two statements differed in status only because we are more confident of the truth of the former. Soon, however, he abandoned this view and took another tack.[3] Since those who assert the analyticity of "All and only men are rational animals" and the synonymy of "man" and "rational animal" often say that the terms "man" and "featherless biped" are coextensive or denote the same individuals while not being synonymous, Goodman examined the nonsynonymy of obviously coextensive terms in the hope of finding a criterion for synonymy, as if he might first learn what nonsynon-

---

[2] See Nelson Goodman, W. V. Quine, and Morton White, "A Triangular Correspondence in 1947," appendix to *A Philosopher's Story*, by Morton White (University Park, Pa., 1999), pp. 337–57.

[3] See Nelson Goodman, "On Likeness of Meaning" (1949), in *Problems and Projects* (New York, 1972), pp. 221–30.

ymy amounts to and then by the back door learn what synonymy is. However, he did not assume that the criterion for synonymy that would emerge by proceeding in this way would permit him to say that the two predicates "man" and "rational animal" are synonymous. On the contrary, the criterion that he finally arrived at led him to say that they are not; indeed it led him to say that *no* two distinct predicates are synonymous and that the best we can say is that they are more or less synonymous, that they are like each other in meaning.

While reflecting on nonsynonymy, Goodman focused on the terms "unicorn" and "centaur" because they clearly have the same denotation or extension—namely, the null extension—while they do not have the same meaning, intension, or connotation. He refused to say that they are not synonymous by virtue of the fact that the attribute of being a centaur is different from the attribute of being a unicorn, since he claimed not to understand what attributes are; but he was willing to say that "unicorn" and "centaur" are not synonymous, because no unicorn-picture is a centaur-picture and no centaur-picture is a unicorn-picture. This statement in a certain respect resembles the claim that they are not synonymous because the attribute of being a unicorn is not identical with the attribute of being a centaur; but for Goodman, pictures have the great advantage of being concrete physical objects, which attributes are not. Like the expression "the attribute of being a unicorn", the expression "the picture of a unicorn" is not what logicians call an extensional context. In other words, if we put the predicate "centaur" for the predicate "unicorn" in the expression "the attribute of being a unicorn", the resulting expression, "the attribute of being a centaur", does not denote the same attribute as "the attribute of being a unicorn" even though "centaur" and "unicorn" denote the same (empty) class; the resulting expression according to some logicians denotes the attribute of being a centaur, which is different from that of being a unicorn. Similarly, we cannot put "centaur" for "unicorn" in the phrase "the picture of a unicorn" and say that both phrases denote the same thing. And because the phrases "picture of a unicorn" and "picture of a centaur" are not extensional contexts, Goodman recommends that we speak in a hyphenated way of unicorn-pictures and of centaur-pictures in order to prevent an unwanted inference from "This is a picture of a unicorn" to "There is a unicorn of which this is a picture" and the analogous inference from "This is a picture of a centaur." We are also prevented by Goodman from saying that we can tell whether something is a unicorn-picture by comparing it with a unicorn, since there are no unicorns with which to compare it. But Goodman goes further and denies that we need show that something is a giraffe-picture by comparing it with a giraffe even though there are giraffes. He insists that we can tell whether something is a unicorn-picture or a giraffe-picture without a criterion or definition of the phrases "unicorn-picture" or "giraffe-picture", just as we can tell whether something is a table or a chair without a definition of "table" or "chair".

Goodman's theory allows us to say what many philosophers believe—namely, that two terms with the same extension, like "unicorn" and "centaur", differ in meaning—but his theory has other consequences that not every philosopher would welcome. For one thing, it does not support the view that "man" and "rational animal" are synonymous. To see why, we must examine Goodman's view more closely. After saying that "centaur" and "unicorn" differ in meaning because no centaur-picture is a unicorn-picture, Goodman calls what is usually called the extension of a term like "unicorn"— the null class—its primary extension, whereas he calls the extension of a term like "unicorn-picture" the secondary extension of "unicorn". Since the primary extension of "unicorn" and that of "centaur" are identical because null, he establishes their nonsynonymy by pointing out that their secondary extensions are different since there are unicorn-pictures that are not centaur-pictures and there are centaur-pictures that are not unicorn-pictures. Next Goodman asks what we should say when two predicates "P" and "Q" refer to odors, in which case there are no P-pictures or Q-pictures. Such predicates present no difficulty, Goodman holds, because the secondary extension of a predicate "Q" contains not only the extension of "Q-picture" but also the extensions of the expressions "Q-diagram", "Q-symbol", and other such compound terms, including "Q-description" This slide from picture to description enlarges the class of secondary extensions of "P" and "Q" to include more than P-pictures and Q-pictures, leading Goodman to say that the phrase "unicorn-description" applies to the linguistic expression "is a unicorn". Moreover, he now can deal with the problem raised by the fact that there are no pictures of pungent odors, for he can say that there is a pungent-odor-description which is not an acrid-odor-description just as he can say that there is a centaur-description which is not a unicorn-description. He says that the expression "a pungent odor that is not an acrid odor" is a pungent odor–description which is not an acrid odor–description, so its existence establishes the nonsynonymy of the predicates "pungent odor" and "acrid odor." He uses this device to show that no two distinct predicates "P" and "Q" are synonymous, since for every pair of such predicates there is an inscription of the form "a P that is not a Q". In sum, Goodman presents two ways of showing the nonsynonymy of two distinct predicates. We may show that their primary extensions differ—as in the case of "dog" and "cat", terms that denote different classes because no dog is a cat. However, when we cannot say that their primary extensions differ—as in the case of "unicorn" and "centaur", which both denote the same (null) class—we can say that their secondary extensions differ by pointing out that there is a unicorn-description which is not a centaur-description, namely, the description "is a unicorn that is not a centaur". This is a description of every unicorn but it is not a description of any centaur.

Such a conclusion might explain why so many analyses offered by analytic philosophers fail to present synonyms, but it does so at a price. It not only leads to saying that "unicorn" and "centaur" are not synonymous, but it also leads to saying that "man" and "rational animal" are not synonymous, that "furze" and "gorse" are not synonymous, and even that "flutist" and "flautist" are not synonymous, since these are all pairs of distinct predicates. This price Goodman is willing to pay since he thinks his conclusion is unusual but not intolerable, just as many philosophical and scientific departures from ordinary language are. Moreover, this conclusion fits with his inclination to say that predicates are at best *alike* in meaning, which in turn fits with the idea that synonymy and therefore analyticity is a matter of degree. It is interesting to note, however, that while the traditionally analytic statement "Every man is a rational animal" is not completely analytic on Goodman's view because "man" is not exactly synonymous with "rational animal", he does not challenge the analyticity of "Every man is a man" since he does not say that "man" is not synonymous with itself. Still, the nonsynonymy of *distinct* predicates is consistent with the great difficulty that philosophers have in showing that predicates such as "man" and "rational animal" are synonymous. It also explains why Goodman denied that the task of philosophy is to find synonyms and why he maintained in *Languages of Art* that philosophers should ask not "What is art?" but rather "When is art?"; from this he concluded that they should be interested not in the mysterious essence of art or the mysterious meaning or intension of "artistic" but rather in what might be called the symptoms or the conditions under which art appears. Here Goodman wished to show that the question "When is art?" is empirical and that art is an ever-changing activity whose so-called nature is not captured in a simple definition or analysis.

This does not mean that the philosopher of art is doomed to silence for fear of trying to capture something ineffable, since Goodman maintains that art is a system of symbols along with science and ordinary language, and therefore he holds that paintings, like predicates, denote and are denoted. According to Goodman, a portrait of Napoleon I denotes an individual and a picture of a robin in a dictionary or guidebook denotes each robin, just as the expression "Napoleon I" denotes Napoleon I and the expression "dictator" denotes Napoleon I, Julius Caesar, and Hitler. By contrast, a picture of Zeus denotes nothing just as the word "Zeus" denotes nothing, and a picture of a unicorn denotes nothing just as the word "unicorn" denotes nothing. Here Goodman applies the device he uses earlier on words, introducing the notions of denotation and exemplification in his discussion of paintings. A picture of Zeus, he says, denotes nothing but exemplifies the expression "Zeus-representation" since the latter is applicable to a picture of Zeus just as the word "Zeus" denotes nothing but exemplifies the expression "Zeus-representation". According to Goodman, a tailor's brown swatch that happens to be square satisfies the predicates "brown" and "square" but does not exemplify or serve as a sample of "square" because the swatch does not refer to squareness. However, the swatch does exemplify or serve as an example of brown. Adopting such a view permitted Goodman to say that Picasso's portrait of Gertrude Stein denoted her while it exemplified monumentality.

I believe, incidentally, that this distinction might be used to elucidate some of John Dewey's remarks about what is *in* a painting and what is external to it, for we may say with Goodman that one of Titian's paintings exemplifies the predicate "sumptuous", since it is sumptuous and also refers to sumptuous things. However, according to Goodman, not every predicate that applies to a painting helps us understand the painting. The predicate "weighs 10 pounds" may apply to a painting but not help us understand it, just as the fact that it was painted by an artist who was born on a Friday may not help us understand it. This stance of Goodman might allow Dewey to distinguish between an intrinsic predicate of a painting and one that is not intrinsic without appealing to the notion of essence, on which Dewey seems to rest in spite of his protestations against it.

Goodman on Art and Science

The similarity between Goodman's views on art and those of Dewey is evident not only in Goodman's technical semantics but also in his more expansive remarks on art. Before he became a professional philosopher he was an art dealer, and he was an enthusiastic collector all his life. Nevertheless, in his *Languages of Art* he remarks, as Dewey does in *Art as Experience*, that he touches only incidentally on questions of value, offers no canons of criticism, and makes no mandatory judgments. But the fact that Goodman's main work in the philosophy of art was a study of what he calls symbols—in which category he includes words, texts, pictures, diagrams, and models— shows how much he resembled Dewey in casting a wide philosophical net that led him to unite his reflections on art and science. Dewey said, "Because objects of art are expressive, they are a language. Rather they are many languages."[4] And Goodman's view that paintings and scientific terms are both symbols shows how much he shared with Dewey, who was so keen to avoid a dualism between art and science. I call attention to these similarities even though Dewey's name does not appear in the index to *Languages of Art* and, so far as I can tell, does not appear in the book.

Like Dewey, Goodman begins his essay "Art and Inquiry" by dissociating himself from the traditional view that the esthetic attitude is passive contemplation uncontaminated by concepts, isolated from all echoes of the past, and exempt from all enterprise.[5] On the contrary, he maintains, it involves making delicate discriminations and discerning subtle relationships. We read a painting, just as we read a poem, he says, because a painting denotes and exemplifies. In this declaration he agrees with Dewey, who says that perception is as creative as art itself. Goodman also agrees with Dewey in refusing to speak of a special esthetic emotion, and like him rejects the idea that the esthetic experience is pleasure read into or "projected" into the object as its property. Moreover, Goodman joins Dewey in criticizing what he calls the "deeply entrenched dichotomy" between the cognitive and the emotive. Goodman rejected this dichotomy because he thought that esthetic and scientific experience are "fundamentally cognitive in character." For this reason, Goodman denies with Dewey that on one side there is "sensation, perception,

[4] John Dewey, *Art as Experience* (New York, 1934), p. 106.
[5] Nelson Goodman, "Art and Inquiry," in *Problems and Projects*, pp. 103–19.

inference, conjecture, all nerveless inspection and investigation, fact, and truth; on the other, pleasure, pain, interest, satisfaction, disappointment, all brainless affective response, liking, and loathing."[6] When we reject this dichotomy, we can see that in esthetic experience the emotions function cognitively and that the work of art is apprehended through the feelings as well as through the senses. Emotion in esthetic experience, according to Goodman, is a means of discerning what predicates apply to a work and therefore what that work exemplifies and expresses. Analogously, I would observe, we may feel the moral obligatoriness of an action, though I hasten to add that Goodman shied away from normative ethics just as he shied away from enunciating canons of esthetic criticism.

I stress the similarity between Goodman's views on art and Dewey's for two main reasons. First, Goodman was opposed to epistemological dualism, as Dewey was. I once remarked that "John Dewey has spent a good part of his life hunting and shooting at dualism: body-mind, theory-practice, percept-concept, value-science, learning-doing, sensation-thought, external-internal,"[7] and I would now add that Goodman shot at these dualisms as well. Second, Dewey encouraged the view that philosophy may examine both science and art as human activities, pointing out that when it does, it can show that they have more in common than is usually supposed. Like Dewey, Goodman was critical of the positivistic dualism between philosophy and science, tried to show what art and science have in common, and obviously departed from the view that philosophy of science is philosophy enough.

How, according to Goodman, are science and art related? Instead of depriving the esthetic experience of emotions, he endowed the understanding with them, remarking: "The fact that emotions participate in cognition no more implies that they are not felt than the

---

[6] Ibid., pp. 105, 107.

[7] Morton White, "The Analytic and the Synthetic: An Untenable Dualism" (1950), reprinted in *Pragmatism and the American Mind: Essays and Reviews in Philosophy and Intellectual History* (New York, 1973), p. 121.

fact that vision helps us discover properties of objects implies that color-sensations do not occur."[8] And like Dewey—who, as we have seen, rejected the idea that esthetic appreciation is a passive affair— Goodman said that it is the opposite of passive absorption in sensations and emotions, yet it by no means cancels them. By viewing esthetic understanding as something that *uses* emotions, we see that in esthetic experience emotions may acquire different features. A dollar earned, saved, or spent is still a dollar, Goodman observes, and by the same token affection eventuating in slavery, frustration, or illumination is still affection. Nevertheless, a dollar bill that is handed to one, a dollar bill that one puts in the bank, and a dollar bill that one pays to a cashier each assumes different properties by turns; similarly, an emotion acquires different properties when used in different ways. Goodman also points out that perception, conception, and feeling intermingle and interact in esthetic experience, and that they are alloyed in a way that may be hard to decompose into emotive and non-emotive elements. He writes: "The same pain (or is it the same?) tells us of ice or fire. Are anger and indignation different feelings or the same feeling under different circumstances?" The point of these rhetorical questions is "that the comparisons, contrasts, and organization involved in the cognitive process often affect the participating emotions. Some may be intensified, as colors are against a complementary ground, or pointed up by subtle rhyming; others may be softened, as are sounds in a louder context."[9] Such an emotion is thus like the dollar bill that goes from *A* to *B* and then from *B* to *C*. Something happens to the bill in the course of these transfers, just as something happens to an emotion like anger when it is felt as indignation.

While discussing the varying cognitive use of emotion in esthetic experience, Goodman observes that it is not present in every esthetic experience nor absent from every non-esthetic experience, just as a symptom of a disease may not be present in all cases nor absent in all

[8] Goodman, "Art and Inquiry," p. 108.
[9] Ibid., p. 109.

cases. "A symptom," he says, "is neither a necessary nor a sufficient condition for, but merely tends in conjunction with other such symptoms to be present in, aesthetic experience."[10] He also calls his symptoms "clues"; and I do not elaborate on his views on them here, because it is necessary to read Goodman carefully to see what they amount to. Goodman lists them as syntactic density, semantic density, relative repleteness, exemplification, and indirect reference; they are symptoms of the symbolizing that occurs when something functions as a work of art. Goodman thinks that one and the same thing, such as a rock or the branch of a tree, may function as a work of art when on display in an art museum but not when it is lying in a forest. This emphasis on function is of course in the pragmatic tradition of James, who thought that what an individual thing is called may vary with the function it is said or thought to have.

Goodman thinks his distinction between the esthetic and the non-esthetic is independent of all considerations of value, since he denies that a characterization of the esthetic requires or provides a definition of esthetic excellence; there are works of art that are not good but nonetheless esthetic. Moreover, Goodman, like Dewey, shies away from using the word "beauty". If the beautiful excludes the ugly, he says trenchantly, it is no measure of esthetic merit, for some of the best pictures are ugly; but if the beautiful may be ugly, then the word "beauty" becomes an alternative and misleading word for esthetic merit. Dewey, as we have seen, often spoke instead of the valued properties of a work of art.

While dealing with esthetic merit, Goodman considers the view that science is judged by its truth whereas art is judged by the satisfaction it gives. But, he asks, what makes a work good or satisfactory? Since being satisfactory is generally assessed relative to function or purpose, and since representation, description, exemplification, and expression are on his view functions of symbols, in asking what con-

---

[10] Nelson Goodman, *Languages of Art: An Approach to a Theory of Symbols* (Indianapolis, 1968), p. 252.

stitutes effective symbolization he asks what purpose such symbolization serves. He rejects three competing answers to the question: that it serves a practical purpose beyond our immediate needs by developing our abilities and techniques to cope with future contingencies, that it is a form of compulsive play, and that its purpose is communication to others. Each of these explanations of *the* purpose of symbolizing is rejected by Goodman because each "distends and distorts a partial truth." Thus he turns to an explanation that is reminiscent of Aristotle's reference to "wonder" and Thorstein Veblen's to "idle curiosity". Here, it must be said, Goodman is not at his most original. Often when he leaves the technical ring in which he is a master and enters one in which logical skill is not enough, his reflections become less arresting or original (but no less important). Goodman says that the primary purpose of symbolizing "is cognition in and for itself"; the practicality, pleasure, compulsion, and communicative utility of symbolizing all depend on the drive of curiosity and the aim of enlightenment, for what compels is the urge to know, what delights is discovery, and communication is secondary to the apprehension and formulation of what is to be communicated. Symbolization is to be judged therefore "by how well it serves the cognitive purpose: by the delicacy of its discriminations and the aptness of its allusions; by the way it works in grasping, exploring, and informing the world; by how it analyzes, sorts, orders, and organizes; by how it participates in the making, manipulation, retention, and transformation of knowledge. Considerations of simplicity and subtlety, power and precision, scope and selectivity, familiarity and freshness, are all relevant and contend with one another; their weighting is relative to our interests, our information, and our inquiry."[11] Goodman's account of how symbolization is to be judged rests on the concept of the cognitive purpose of symbolization; but he says little about how we show what *the* purpose of symbolizing

[11] Goodman, "Art and Inquiry," pp. 114–15.

is, just as Quine says little about how we show that *the* purpose of science is prediction. Showing that *something* is *the purpose of something* is presumably an empirical enterprise for Goodman, so he may be fairly asked what his evidence is for believing that symbolization has whatever purpose he assigns to it. Does he think that we know that it has that purpose without argument or criterion, as he thinks we know that something is a giraffe-picture?

I ask this question because a great deal rides on Goodman's view of the purpose of symbolization. He tells us that symbolization is *to be* judged by measuring its cognitive efficacy, and therefore that the excellence of an esthetic object is not attributable only to works of art. Beginning with a general idea of cognitive excellence or the idea of the cognitive efficacy of symbols, he says that esthetic merit is such excellence in any symbolic functioning that, by its particular constellation of attributes, qualifies as esthetic. In other words, cognitive efficacy or excellence is a genus of which the cognitive efficacy of an esthetic object is a species. But there is, on Goodman's view, another species of cognitive excellence, namely, science. Goodman is aware that he may be asked whether, in judging works of art by standards of cognitive excellence, he has overlooked the fact that in science, unlike art, the ultimate test is truth. In response he says that truth *by itself* matters very little in science. The truths of science, he says, must be answers to significant or important questions, so truth is not enough; it is at most a necessary condition for being scientific. But even this concedes too much, he maintains, since scientific laws are seldom quite true; experimental scientists record laboratory data that do not accord with the smooth curves they draw when they graph their results. Goodman also declares that truth is not among the criteria scientists use when they choose between rival hypotheses, since scientists have no direct access to their truth. Rather, Goodman says with James, they come to attribute truth to hypotheses by gauging their simplicity, their strength, and, Goodman might have added with James, Tarski, and Quine, the degree to which they keep long-held beliefs in place. Scientists, Goodman says with

James, do not try to mirror so-called facts since there are no such entities that "correspond" in any clear sense to very abstract hypotheses. Implicit in this position is the holistic view that a scientific theory is a conjunction some of whose components are said to be true because they contribute to the efficacy of the conjunction in organizing experience, and not because they mirror or copy facts.

Goodman tries to lead us to his conclusion about the relation between art and science by initially arguing that art is like science in many ways and then arguing that the science is like art in many ways. First he says that an artistic symbol may be viewed cognitively because, like a linguistic predicate, it refers by virtue of denoting or by exemplifying. Then he says that the truth of a hypothesis is not a necessary or a sufficient condition for its being incorporated into science since we have no direct access to truth. He adds that truth is a matter of fit—"fit with a body of theory, and fit of hypothesis and theory to the data at hand and facts to be encountered"—and that "goodness of fit takes a two-way adjustment—of theory to facts and of facts to theory—with the double aim of comfort and a new look." Here, without citing William James, he comes to a Jamesian conclusion about science; and once he has reached this point, he declares triumphantly: "But such fitness, such aptness in conforming to and reforming our knowledge and our world, is equally relevant for the aesthetic symbol." Goodman writes: "Truth and its aesthetic counterpart amount to appropriateness under different names. If we speak of hypotheses but not of works of art as true, that is because we reserve the terms true and false for symbols in sentential form. I do not say this difference is negligible, but it is specific rather than generic, a difference in field of application rather than in formula, and marks no schism between the scientific and the aesthetic".[12] His point is that there is a genus called "appropriate symbols" which has

---

[12] Ibid., pp. 117–18. Compare this last quotation with William James's remark in Lecture II of his *Pragmatism* ([ed. Fredson Bowers and Ignas K. Skrupskelis] [Cambridge, Mass., 1975], p. 42): "truth is *one species of good*, and not, as is usually supposed, a category distinct from good, and coordinate with it."

at least two species—appropriate scientific symbols that are sentences, and appropriate artistic symbols that are not sentences—and
that we happen to apply the word "true" to the first species but not
to the second. Analogously we say, I suppose, that a group of wolves
is a pack, a group of lions is a pride, and a group of geese is a gaggle,
yet these are all groups even though we give them different names.
Similarly, a painting and a sentence may both be cognitively appropriate, even though the former is said to have esthetic merit whereas
the latter is called true. We may say, as Goodman says—once again,
in the spirit of Dewey's anti-dualism—that "the difference between
art and science is not that between feeling and fact, intuition and
inference, delight and deliberation, synthesis and analysis, sensation
and cerebration, concreteness and abstraction, passion and action,
mediacy and immediacy, or truth and beauty, but rather a difference
in domination of certain specific characteristics of symbols." This is
Deweyan and a far cry from Quine, who approved of "the deep old
duality of thought and feeling, of the head and the heart, the cortex
and the thalamus, the words and the music."[13]

Although Goodman does not venture into moral philosophy, I
think that ethical symbols may also be regarded as cognitively appropriate; we may speak of the cognitive efficacy of ethical symbols
as we speak of the cognitive efficacy of esthetic symbols and those
of natural science. In other words, I believe that cognitively appropriate ethical symbols constitute another species of Goodman's (and
James's) genus.[14] Just as Goodman maintains that the noblest scientific laws are seldom quite true and that discrepancies are often over-
ridden by scientists in the interest of breadth or power or simplicity,
so we may say that the noblest moral principles are seldom quite
true and that moral thinkers also ride over discrepancies while they
seek breadth, power, or simplicity. And just as we say that we do not
have mirrored access to truth in physics or chemistry, so we may say
the same thing about ethics with perhaps greater assurance. In eth-

[13] Goodman, "Art and Inquiry," pp. 108, 118; W. V. Quine, "On the Nature of Moral
Values," in *Theories and Things* (Cambridge, Mass., 1981), p. 55.
[14] I develop this view in chapter 10.

ics, furthermore, truth is a matter of a belief's fitting in with our other beliefs, with our sensory experiences, and with our feelings of obligation, and such a fit involves a two-way adjustment between belief on the one hand and these varieties of experience on the other. It may also be argued that the cognitive efficacy of formal logic is measured similarly; and once we arrive at this conclusion, we see that logical, physical, ethical, and esthetic symbols constitute different species of one genus of cognitively efficacious symbols. For this reason we would do well to abandon the idea that logic, physics, ethics, and esthetics use four radically different methods of supporting claims of cognitive appropriateness. We would also do well to recognize that philosophy of culture is a study of all these modes of discourse, and perhaps of others.

Although Goodman, like Quine, had little interest in ethics, I think that Goodman's genus of cognitively appropriate symbols was wider than he may have thought. I also think that the holism of Quine and Tarski was wider than they thought, and in the following chapters I try to show why. My aim there, as in earlier parts of this study, is to broaden the scope of holistic pragmatism so that it may be regarded as a philosophy of culture. In doing so I shall maintain that Tarski and Quine built better than they knew. By expanding the horizon of philosophy even further, we do something of which the ur-pragmatists James and Dewey would have approved.

IX

Rule, Ruling, and Prediction in the Law

Hart v. Holmes

Historians of philosophy often neglect the holistic strain in James's philosophy of science as well as an interesting though brief statement in his *Pragmatism* in which he applies his holism to the law. In Lecture VII he says that scientific truth grafts itself on previous truth—that is, on the older stock of truths to which he had referred in an earlier lecture—and it modifies previous truth in the process. He then adds that law similarly grafts itself on previous law. "Given previous law and a novel case," James notes, "and the judge will twist them into fresh law," just as the scientist begins with a conjunction of previous truths, encounters fresh facts, and incorporates fresh truths or revises the old.[1] A decade before these words of James were published, his boyhood friend, Justice Oliver Wendell Holmes, Jr., had delivered a speech in Boston called "The Path of the Law" in which he expressed a view of judges and the law that resembles James's. As a fellow anti-rationalist, Holmes rejected the idea that the law is "a system of reason, . . . a deduction from principles of ethics or admit-

---

[1] William James, *Pragmatism*, [ed. Fredson Bowers and Ignas K. Skrupskelis] (Cambridge, Mass., 1975), p. 116.

ted axioms or what not, which may or may not coincide with the [judicial] decisions," declaring in one of his best-known statements: "The prophecies of what the courts will do in fact, and nothing more pretentious, are what I mean by the law."[2]

Holmes's View of Law and Hart's Criticism of It

Before Holmes offered his now famous answer to the question "What constitutes the law?" he prepared the reader for the context of the expression "the law" by saying that when we study law we are studying a well-known profession. And, he continues, the reason why it is a profession, or why people will pay lawyers to argue for them or to advise them about what judges will do, "is that in societies like ours the command of the public force is intrusted to the judges in certain cases, and the whole power of the state will be put forth, if necessary, to carry out their judgments and decrees." "People," he says, "want to know under what circumstances and how far they will run the risk of coming against what is so much stronger than themselves, and hence it becomes a business to find out when this danger is to be feared. The object of our study, then, is prediction, the prediction of the incidence of the public force through the in-strumentality of the courts" (p. 173). Holmes adds that such a pre-diction is what a bad man pays a lawyer to make; but he need not have denied that an inquisitive man, whether good or bad, might pay a lawyer to tell him whether the court will or will not order him to do certain things. We must also keep in mind that if, as Holmes maintained, the lawyer makes predictions to his client of what courts are likely to do in fact, it would be hard for a lawyer to make such predictions merely by knowing the rules of law that the judge would be likely to apply to the case in question. In predicting what a judge will decree, the lawyer will have to know more about him than that.

---

[2] Oliver Wendell Holmes, "The Path of the Law," in *Collected Legal Papers* (New York, 1920), pp. 172, 173. This essay is hereafter cited parenthetically in the text.

In the twentieth century, many legal thinkers criticized these views of Holmes, but I want to focus on the reaction to them of H.L.A. Hart, the Oxford philosopher of law, in order to clarify and at places try to improve on what Holmes said. Hart disagreed not only with Holmes's view that the law consists merely of predictions of what the courts will do, but also with his narrower view that we should regard the lawyer's client as a bad man if we wish to view the law properly. It seems clear that Holmes should not have denied that a good man may pay his lawyer for a prediction out of curiosity rather than fear, since it is obvious that a lawyer may predict to a good man that the court will *permit* him to draw a will of a certain kind and thereby grant him a power. And when she predicts this, she will in effect tell her client how the public force may be used in his interest and not to thwart his desires. This version of the predictive theory is compatible with Hart's view that the law not only says what people have a legal duty or obligation to do but also what they have a legal right or power to do; and had he omitted the "bad man" theory from "The Path of the Law", admirers of Holmes would have been spared the need to answer certain less serious objections to his view. Bad men pay for legal predictions more often than good men do because bad men consult lawyers more often, but I think Holmes should have recognized that lawyers are paid by good and bad men to predict, not that they are paid to predict by bad men only. Furthermore, Holmes said in "The Path of the Law" that his predictive theory could be applied not only to the concept of legal duty but also to that of legal right (p. 169), and he stated in his essay "Natural Law": "For legal purposes a right is only the hypostasis of a prophecy—the imagination of a substance supporting the fact that the public force will be brought to bear upon those who do things said to contravene it."[3] In telling a client about his rights, the lawyer will be telling him how the law will help him, namely, by warning others who might wish to contravene those rights.

---

[3] Oliver Wendell Holmes, "Natural Law," in *Collected Legal Papers*, p. 313.

One of Hart's central objections to Holmes's view was that saying that a person has a legal obligation to do something does not *mean the same* as saying that he will be punished if he does not perform that act. Hart writes: "If it were true that the statement that a person had [a legal] obligation *meant* [my emphasis] that *he* was likely to suffer in the event of disobedience, it would be a contradiction to say that he had an obligation, e.g. to report for military service but that, owing to the fact that he had escaped from the jurisdiction, or had successfully bribed the police or the court, there was not the slightest chance of his being caught or made to suffer. In fact, there is no contradiction in saying this, and such statements are often made and understood."[4] Since Hart held the predictive theory of law to be an assertion of synonymy, he thought he could refute it merely by showing that the conjunction "Jones had a legal obligation to report for military service but he did not suffer when he did not report" is *not contradictory*—a dubious sort of philosophical claim that the reader now knows has been seriously criticized.[5] Hart, like many philosophers in the middle of the twentieth century, never shed the tendency of earlier analytic philosophers to rest on a debatable notion of synonymy when rejecting certain philosophical views. However, Holmes opened himself to that kind of criticism when he spoke loosely, as he often did, about meaning and was therefore taken by many readers like Hart to have held that "Jones has a legal obligation to report for military service" *is* synonymous with a predictive statement about judicial behavior.

A more friendly interpretation of Holmes would *not* have him saying that the statement "Jones has a legal obligation to report for military service" has the same meaning or intension as a predictive

---

[4] H.L.A. Hart, *The Concept of Law* (Oxford, 1961), p. 82.

[5] See Nelson Goodman, W. V. Quine, and Morton White, "A Triangular Correspondence in 1947," appendix to *A Philosopher's Story*, by Morton White (University Park, Pa., 1999), pp. 337–57. Also see Nelson Goodman, "On Likeness of Meaning," in *Problems and Projects* (New York, 1972), pp. 221–30; Morton White, "The Analytic and the Synthetic: An Untenable Dualism," in *Pragmatism and the American Mind: Essays and Reviews in Philosophy and Intellectual History* (New York, 1973), pp. 121–37; and W. V. Quine, "Two Dogmas of Empiricism," in *From a Logical Point of View: Nine Logico-Philosophical Essays* (Cambridge, 1953), pp. 20–46.

conditional statement. In being more friendly, however, one must overlook some of Holmes's questionable semantic declarations, such as his statement in "The Path of the Law" that "The duty to keep a contract at common law means a prediction that you must pay damages if you do not keep it—and nothing else." One must disregard this philosophically incongruous claim that a legal duty "means" a prediction, and Holmes's equally incongruous statement that a legal duty "is nothing but a prediction" (pp. 169, 175). Would Holmes have avoided Hart's objection by saying, only as a matter of fact, that a person has a legal duty to keep a contract if and only if failure to keep it will cause the person harm? No, because even this logically weaker assertion would expose him to Hart's sort of counterexample had Holmes not specified (as he did) that the harm in question must be court-ordered. Otherwise Holmes would have been forced to say that if it is true that a woman will be harmed if she does not hand over a diamond ring to a gunman, she has a legal duty to hand it over.

As I have indicated, however, Holmes characterized the lawyer's prediction as "a prediction that if a man does or omits certain things he will be made to suffer in this or that way *by judgment of the court*" (p. 169; my emphasis). Therefore he distinguished between predicting harm at the direction of a court and predicting harm administered by a gunman because he thought that the court is a legal authority whereas a gunman is not. Yet Holmes said little in "The Path of the Law" about the notion of legal authority, perhaps because he was interested not in what he called a "useless quintessence of all legal systems" but in "an accurate anatomy of one" (pp. 196–97). If Holmes were asked how predicting a court's or a judge's ruling differs from a gunman's threat, he might have said that although he did not define the word "judge" explicitly, he knew a judge when he saw one, and so could distinguish harm ordered by a judge from harm administered by a gunman. Perhaps he would have said in philosophical parlance that he could define "judge" and "gunman" ostensively; but in failing to discuss the concept of a judge or a legal authority at greater length, he failed to say enough about what judges do. Holmes said a good deal about why we pay lawyers, but since he thought clients pay them to predict what judges will do, he would have done well to say more about why we pay judges and therefore make clearer than he did why a predicting lawyer's defense of his *prediction* of a decree is different from a judge's defense of his *decree*.

The Judge's Reasoning and the Predicting Lawyer's Reasoning

Holmes suggests in places that one task of a judge is to issue a logically singular ruling or decree that an individual such as Jones has a legal obligation to report for military service, and that in simple cases the judge defends a singular ruling by citing a general rule which says that every individual of a certain kind is legally obligated to report for military service, as well as a singular statement of fact that Jones meets that description. But Holmes should have emphasized more strongly that while the judge issues and defends a singular legal *ruling* or decree, a client's lawyer issues and defends a prediction that the judge will issue that ruling. Holmes should have made clearer than he did that the lawyer's prediction of a decree should not be confused with the judge's decree, since no one is legally obligated to act in accordance with a lawyer's predictive statement.

In some ways the predicting lawyer, according to Holmes, is like an accountant who says that the Internal Revenue Service will rule that her client is legally obligated to pay a certain amount of tax. The accountant predicts the bottom line at which the IRS will arrive, and, by analogy, the lawyer predicts the bottom line at which the judge will arrive. The accountant does not usually bother her client with the tax law that will lead the IRS to its bottom line; nor does the lawyer usually bother his client with the legal reasoning that the judge will use to reach his decree. There is also an analogy between a lawyer and a family physician. Why do we pay a general practitioner? What do we want her to tell us? Usually, we want to know what we should do to get rid of or to ward off a cough, an attack of indigestion, or a pain in the back. When a physician recommends a medicine or an exercise, she makes a prediction that if you do such-and-such, so-and-so will happen. Do we normally pay the physician to recite the laws of medical technology or science she rests on when prescribing what she prescribes? No. Do we usually pay her to present the biomedical theory that supports her recommendation? No. A few patients may be interested in paying for that sort of information, but most legal clients will not be after they hear the lawyer's hourly billing rates. They merely seek a prediction of how the court will rule, and that is the bottom line that the lawyer predicts when he says that a judge will issue the decree "Jones has a legal obligation to report for military service."

However, there is at least one important difference between a prediction that a doctor makes to a patient and one that a lawyer makes to his client. A doctor may predict the physiological action of a pill, but the lawyer predicts the deliberate ruling of a judge who is a human being. And because the lawyer seeks to predict the decree of a judge who presumably follows a legal rule, the lawyer may also predict which rule of law the judge will follow. Moreover, when the lawyer predicts a judge's decree, he will rely not only on his beliefs about what rule a judge will follow but also on beliefs about the judge's learning, the judge's logical acuity and honesty, and sometimes the judge's own moral beliefs. If the lawyer is worth his fee, he will use every scrap of information that he thinks will help him predict the judge's ruling, just as a reliable tax accountant will; so it should be emphasized that the predicting lawyer and the predicting accountant are primarily empirical students of the behavior of government officials, whereas a judge who issues a decree does not make a prediction about himself when he issues it.

Holmes not only *need not* have said that the judge's decree is synonymous with the lawyer's prediction of that decree but *should not* have said that they are synonymous in the way that "Jones is a bachelor" and " Jones is an unmarried male adult" are often said to be. If this is not obvious, its truth can be shown by pointing out that a judge defends his decree by means of an argument which differs from that offered by the lawyer in support of his prediction of the judge's ruling. The Holmesian lawyer views the judge much as a psychologist does, since the lawyer is paid to predict what decree the judge will issue, but *the judge* is not paid to be a self-analyzing psychologist who *predicts* what ruling he himself will issue. He *makes a ruling* and often defends it by resting on a holistic conjunction of legal rules, factual beliefs, and sometimes moral beliefs; in contrast, the lawyer defends his *prediction* by *mentioning* those rules and beliefs that will appear in the judge's reasoning, not by using them as premises in defense of his, the lawyer's, prediction.

The Lawyer's Prediction and the Judge's Decree

How, then, *are* the lawyer's prediction of what a judge will decree and the judge's actual decree related if they are not synonymous? Since Hart mentions that the judge might have been bribed, Holmes might have said in anticipation of this criticism that the able predicting lawyer will take this possibility into account when making his prediction of the judge's decree. If the lawyer believes that the judge has been bribed, the lawyer will probably predict the decree "Jones *does not* have a legal obligation to report for military service." Moreover, as I have already stated, the judge's decree and the lawyer's prediction of the decree are not related to each other as the factually equivalent statements "Jones has a kidney" and "Jones has a heart" are, because it is not true that a person *has* a legal obligation to report for military service if and only if the judge *will* decree that he has a legal obligation to report for military service. Holmes should not say that Jones now has a legal obligation to report for military service if and only if the judge *will* decree tomorrow that he has that obligation; he should say that Jones has that obligation if and only if the judge *has* decreed that he has that obligation. A prediction of a decree is like a prediction that it will rain tomorrow, and we do not know today that the latter prediction is true. If one says with Holmes that a person has a legal obligation if and only if he is decreed by a judge to have that obligation, one must be careful about one's tenses. If Jones's having the obligation depends on a judge's decreeing that he has it, then Jones has that obligation after but not *before* the decree has been rendered. Before the decree has been rendered, the lawyer should not say that Jones *has* a legal obligation; he should say that he *will have* that obligation when and if the judge has issued a certain decree.

Unlike Holmes, Hart thinks that Jones may have a legal obligation to report for military service no matter what the judge *says*, which means in Holmes's words that Hart holds that the law may or may not coincide with judicial decisions. Therefore, Hart should not only deny that "Jones has a legal obligation to report for military service" is synonymous with the *prediction* that a judge will issue that as a decree, but should also deny that Jones has a legal obligation to report for military service if and only if a judge *has decreed* "Jones has a legal obligation to report for military service." Unlike Holmes, Hart seems to think that there may be a true fact of legal obligation that is independent of the judge's decree; and we may write the statement that records this so-called fact in capital letters, "JONES HAS A LEGAL OBLIGATION TO REPORT FOR MILITARY SERVICE," to distinguish it from the judge's identically worded decree, which we may write in lowercase letters. Hart denies that JONES HAS A LEGAL OBLIGATION TO REPORT FOR MILITARY SERVICE if and only if Judge William has decreed "Jones has a legal obligation to report for military service", because Hart thinks that the left-hand side of the expression "if and only if" may be true when the right-hand side is false—for example, when Judge William has been bribed. That is why the capitalized sentence and the lowercase decree are not related as "Jones has a heart" and "Jones has a kidney" are. As a matter of fact, all and only animals with hearts have kidneys, but in fact not all judicial decisions coincide with their Hartian capitalized counterparts.

Hart's view resembles that of a baseball fan who says that it is not a necessary and sufficient condition *for being a strike* that the umpire has called out "Strike!" because the fan sometimes asserts "THAT'S A STRIKE" when the umpire decrees "That's a ball". By contrast, in a view like Holmes's, a pitch is a strike if and only if it has been decreed to be a strike by the umpire; for this reason, Holmes maintains that the client merely wants to know what the judge—the counterpart of the umpire—will decree, and pays the lawyer to predict that decree.[6] According to Holmes, Jones does not care "two straws" (p. 173) about whether he has a Hartian legal obligation expressed in capitals that is independent of the judge's lowercase decree that may send him to jail. Holmes and Jones merely want to know whether *the decree* will be "Jones has a legal duty to report for military service" or "Jones does not have a legal duty to report for military service". In that case, Hart's conjunctive statement, "JONES HAS A LEGAL OBLIGATION TO REPORT FOR MILITARY SERVICE but the bribed judge decreed 'Jones had no legal obligation to report for military service' ", will be of no interest to Jones *or* to Holmes, because neither of them cares two straws about the statement before the "but". They care only about the lowercase judicial *decree* of non-obligation, because only that will directly influence the client's behavior.

All of this suggests that Holmes and the client regard the lawyer's prediction of the decree as *a sign or signal* that the judge's decree will be made. The client trusts and pays the lawyer as he trusts and pays a reliable meteorologist, and therefore may say, "The fact that Clarence Darrow *predicts* that the judge will issue decree *D* tomorrow is a sign to me that the judge *will* issue decree *D* tomorrow"—

---

[6] Maybe a better illustration is the case in which the fan says "That's an error" and the official scorer decrees that the play is not an error. The scorer's decree determines whether or not a player has made an error.

which is like saying "Those clouds are a sign that rain will come," or "The meteorologist's saying 'It will be 90° tomorrow' is a sign that it will be 90° tomorrow." The client bets that the lawyer's prediction is correct, and this view makes peace between Hart and Holmes, but only up to a point. Hart might have welcomed it, because it seems to vindicate his view that "JONES HAS A LEGAL OBLIGATION TO REPORT FOR MILITARY SERVICE" is neither synonymous with, nor true if and only if the decree "Jones has a legal obligation to report for military service" has been issued. Nor does it stand in that relation to the lawyer's prediction, "Judge William will decree 'Jones has an obligation to report for military service' ". Holmes might have welcomed this result because it does not commit him to saying that there is a Hartian fact of legal obligation that is expressed in capitals. However, it avoids saying that a legal obligation *is* a prediction, or that it *means* a prediction, both of which are obvious violations of philosophical grammar on Holmes's part. According to the Holmesian lawyer and his client, we can read a judge's decree and a lawyer's prediction of that decree; and if Hart were to insist that there is a fact of legal obligation which is independent of the decree, Holmes would have replied that the client does not pay the lawyer to report it or that there is no such fact.

Two Uses of "Law"

At first blush it would seem that Hart disregarded a contention of Holmes in the passage that concludes with his famous statement from "The Path of the Law" quoted above: "Take the fundamental question, What constitutes the law? You will find some text writers telling you that it is something different from what is decided by the courts of Massachusetts or England, that it is a system of reason, that it is a deduction from principles of ethics or admitted axioms or what not, which may or may not coincide with the decisions. But if we take the view of our friend the bad man we shall find that he does not care two straws for the axioms or deductions, but that he does want to know what the Massachusetts or English courts are likely to do in fact. I am much of his mind. The prophecies of what the courts will do in fact, and nothing more pretentious, are what I mean by the law" (pp. 172–73).

If Hart had been confronted with this passage, he might have replied that he did not "take the view" of Holmes, because in asserting a legal obligation he was not interested in saying why we pay lawyers—he does not focus on the context in which the phrase "has a legal obligation" is used by Holmes. Hart might say that unlike a lawyer, a judge who asks "Does Jones have a legal duty to report for military service?" is not asking himself to *predict* his own decree. In saying that the law is not understood *by the paying client* to be a system of reason or a deduction from principles of ethics or admitted axioms or whatnot, Holmes should have allowed that *the judge*, who makes and derives his decree from a conjunction of statutes or legal rules and other statements, "takes" a different view of the law. And Hart may have been taking a view that is like the judge's view of the law, rather than that of the client and his lawyer. The fact that Hart and Holmes focus on different contexts of "law" was consonant with Holmes's general observation: "It is not true that in practice (and I know no reason why theory should disagree with the facts) a given word or even a given collocation of words has one meaning and no other. A word generally has several meanings, even in the dictionary. You have to consider the sentence in which it stands to decide which of those meanings it bears in the particular case[.]"[7] Why, then, shouldn't Hart have granted that in taking the view of the bill-paying client, Holmes was investigating the word "law" as used by the client whereas Hart, by taking the view of the judge, was investigating a different use of it? The lawyer is paid to predict the judge's

---

[7] Oliver Wendell Holmes, "The Theory of Legal Interpretation," in *Collected Legal Papers*, p. 203.

decree, but the judge, Hart might say, is paid to issue a lowercase decree that he thinks will coincide with a capitalized statement of legal obligation.

Since Holmes began "The Path of the Law" by indicating an interest in finding out why we pay lawyers and concluded by saying that we pay them to predict what the courts will do to us, he should not have maintained dogmatically that he had answered the question "What constitutes the law?" and should not have suggested that there was no other context in which "the law" referred to something else. In other words, he should have allowed that as used by a judge (by contrast to a lawyer and his client), the phrase "the law" might refer to something else. Had he said he was trying to answer the question "What does a client who is contemplating an action of a certain kind pay a lawyer to tell him?", his view would not have been open to many of the objections discussed earlier. He should have made clearer than he did that in his view the expression "the law" in only *one* of its uses refers to prophecies by lawyers of rulings by a judge in a court. But even if Holmes held that there are no Hartian facts of legal obligation and that only judicial decrees "really" express legal obligations, Holmes should not have confused the lawyer's predictions of those decrees with the decrees themselves, since a person is not punished for violating a prediction. In saying that legal obligations are expressed only in judicial decrees, he failed to recognize that a deciding judge may view a legal obligation in a manner different from that in which the client and his lawyer view it.

"The Path of the Law" and Holmes's Dissent in Lochner v. New York

Because Holmes was so eager to treat the notion of legal duty with what he called cynical acid, he wrote that it might be "a gain if every word of moral significance would be banished from the law altogether, and other words adopted which would convey legal ideas uncolored by anything outside the law." And it was in trying to rid the law of moral language that he came to treat the lawyer's task as that of an empirical *predictor* of decrees of obligation, a mode of looking at law that he said "stinks in the nostrils of those who think it advantageous to get as much ethics into the law as they can" (p. 175). This approach would fit with his declaration in "The Path of the Law" that legal rules are generalized prophecies, and that "the primary rights and duties with which jurisprudence busies itself . . . *are nothing but* prophecies" (p. 168; my emphasis). This statement is questionable not only because it identifies rights and duties with prophecies but also for the following reasons. If the judge appeals to a rule that every person of a certain kind and in a certain condition has a certain legal obligation, and therefore orders what is *to be done* by one person of that kind, it is hard to see how that rule can be construed as a generalized prophecy of a decree. It does not say that everyone of a certain kind and in a certain condition *will be decreed* by a judge or by anyone else to have a legal duty to do something, but rather that such a person *has* a legal duty to do something. If legal rules were generalized prophecies of decrees, then the judge, like the lawyer on Holmes's view, would defend his decree of obligation empirically by appealing to one factual premise according to which every person of a certain kind and in a certain condition will be *decreed* to have that obligation, and to another factual premise according to which Jones is of that kind and in that condition. The judge in that case would be said to deduce the statement that Jones *will be decreed* by him *to have* a certain obligation rather than his legal decree, which rules that Jones *has* that obligation; and this is inconsistent with saying that the judge *makes* or issues his decrees of obligation rather than predictions of those decrees.

To complicate matters, Holmes does not always say that the judge is a thoroughly empirical investigator who assumes only generalized prophecies and derives singular prophecies from them. To show this, I turn to his famous dissent in the 1905 Supreme Court case *Lochner v. New York*. I recognize that this differs from the case involving our imaginary Jones, but I want to emphasize that in his *Lochner* dissent

Holmes seems to hold that judges sometimes support their rulings by appealing to moral premises as well as to statements of fact and generalized prophecies. Though here the Court majority did not rule that a person like Jones had a legal duty, there is a similarity between their ruling that a New York State law was unconstitutional and a ruling that Jones had a legal obligation, inasmuch as the former says that because New York State had no constitutional right to have enacted that law it therefore had a legal obligation not to have enacted it. If a lawyer had predicted the Court's decision, he would have mentioned or *referred* to a moral premise that Holmes thought was assumed by the majority in defense of its ruling, but the lawyer himself would not have *assumed* that moral premise in supporting his prediction.

In *Lochner*, the Supreme Court struck down as unconstitutional a New York law that provided for a ten-hour day and a sixty-hour week in the baking industry, and in his dissent Holmes announced in much-quoted words that "General propositions do not decide concrete cases." He continued, "The decision will depend on a judgment or intuition more subtle than any articulate major premise."[8] I think his point was that the majority depended on an unarticulated *moral* premise that he articulated and then declared unacceptable because the Constitution did not contain it or imply it. He remarked sardonically that the Fourteenth Amendment did not enact Herbert Spencer's *Social Statics*, adding that the moral principle—which he misleadingly calls economic—upon which the majority rested, namely, "The liberty of the citizen to do as he likes so long as he does not interfere with the liberty of others to do the same", was "a shibboleth" or a view held only by one group in American society.[9] That Holmes regarded Spencer's shibboleth as moral in spite of calling it economic may be seen more easily if we read the version of it quoted in "The Path of the Law," which is plainly moral and not economic: "Every man has a right to do as he wills, provided he

---

[8] *Lochner v. New York*, 198 U.S. 45, 76 (1905).
[9] Ibid. at 75.

interferes not with a like right on the part of his neighbors" (p. 182). Surely this is not an economic principle; and so I think Holmes said in his *Lochner* dissent that if this assumed shibboleth about *moral* rights had been made explicit by the majority, its defense of its ruling would have been seen to be unconstitutional, because a constitution "is made for people of fundamentally differing views" on moral issues[10]—meaning, I suppose, that a shibboleth like Spencer's should not be used in support of the Court's decision. Yet by calling Spencer's moral shibboleth an unarticulated premise of the majority of the Court, Holmes showed that he believed that judges sometimes do use moral premises—however inarticulately—in arriving at their rulings, and therefore do not argue *only* from factual premises and legal rules conceived as generalized prophecies.

Although Holmes said in *Lochner* that the Court should not have rested on a moral shibboleth in declaring the New York statute unconstitutional, he also said in "The Path of the Law" that "judges themselves have failed adequately to recognize their duty of weighing considerations of social advantage. The duty is inevitable, and the result of the often proclaimed judicial aversion to deal with such considerations is simply to leave the very ground and foundation of judgments inarticulate, and often unconscious" (p. 184).[11] This statement supports the idea that Holmes did not complain in his *Lochner* dissent because the majority rested on a *moral* principle; he complained because it rested on a moral principle that was a shibboleth. Indeed, in "The Path of the Law" his words seemed to anticipate this view: "I cannot but believe that if the training of lawyers [presumably lawyers who become judges] led them habitually to consider more definitely and explicitly the social advantage on which the rule they lay down must be justified, they sometimes would hesitate where now they are confident, and see that they were taking sides upon debatable and often burning questions" (p. 184). I take this to be compatible with his position that if the *Lochner* majority

[10] Ibid. at 76.
[11] I will not linger over Holmes's use of the word "duty" here. Is it legal or moral?

had followed this advice, they would have seen that they were taking sides by resting on a moral belief that was not widely accepted. But if they had instead rested on a judgment of the value to society of a law mandating no more than a ten-hour day and a sixty-hour week, they would also be resting on a moral belief—yet this latter moral belief would not, in Holmes's view, be a shibboleth.

Holmes thought that Spencer's moral shibboleth was mistakenly used by the Court in *Lochner* when interpreting the Fourteenth Amendment's declaration that no state shall deprive any person of the liberty or right to contract—a liberty or right that was supposed by the Court majority to be curtailed when New York State required a company to demand no more than a ten-hour day and a sixty-hour week from its workers. Not only did Holmes seem to say the majority rested on a moral premise that was a shibboleth, but he argued that the state constitutions of his day implicitly rejected that shibboleth when they passed school laws, Sunday laws, usury laws, and laws prohibiting lotteries. Such laws, he said, interfere with a citizen's Spencerian liberty to do as he pleases without interfering with the liberty of others to do the same, simply because such laws "tak[e] his money for purposes thought desirable, whether he likes it or not." Such state laws, Holmes implied, were not unconstitutional, because a court could not reasonably say that such statutes went against a moral belief that was "dominant" in the country. Holmes maintained: "I think the word 'liberty,' in the 14th Amendment, is perverted when it is held [as by the Court majority] to prevent the natural outcome of a dominant opinion, unless it can be said that a rational and fair man necessarily would admit that the statute proposed would infringe fundamental principles as they have been understood by the traditions of our people and our law." Then Holmes concluded, "It does not need research to show that no such sweeping condemnation can be passed upon the statute before us. A reasonable man might think it a proper measure on the score of health. Men whom I certainly could not pronounce unreasonable would uphold it as a first instalment of a general regulation of the hours of work".[12]

When Holmes appealed to what a rational and *fair* man necessarily would or would not say, he used a *moral* belief to support the constitutionality of the statute that his brethren had declared unconstitutional. So, while in Holmes's view the majority of the Court covertly used Spencer's moral premise when it determined that the New York law infringed the employer's right to contract, that *covert* premise was no more and no less moral than Holmes's *overt* statement that no rational and just man would necessarily say that a statute requiring no more than a ten-hour day and sixty-hour week in bakeries "would infringe fundamental principles as they have been understood by the traditions of our people and our law." It would appear, therefore, that in Holmes's view a judge may appeal to a moral principle which is a "dominant opinion" that a reasonable man might think proper, but not to a shibboleth. Therefore, what distinguished Holmes's argument in *Lochner* from that of the majority of the Court was, among other things, his position that one moral belief was acceptable and was not a shibboleth whereas the majority unconsciously rested on a belief that was not acceptable and was a shibboleth. This was compatible with Holmes's statement in "The Path of the Law" that "behind the logical forms lies a judgment as to the relative *worth* and importance of competing legislative grounds, often an inarticulate and unconscious judgment, it is true, and yet the very root and nerve of the whole proceeding" (p. 181; my emphasis).

Once we grant Holmes's point in "The Path of the Law" that opposing judges often rest on judgments of moral worth, we can see why a lawyer who tried to predict a judge's decree in a case like *Lochner* would have been helped by knowing what the judge's moral preferences or judgments of worth were. However, that a predicting lawyer thinks that a court assumes such a moral premise does not

[12] *Lochner v. New York*, 75, 76.

mean that the lawyer himself assumes the moral premise in grounding his prediction. Knowing that a judge is a moral pacifist might help a lawyer predict what a judge would decree in Jones's case, but the lawyer's statement that a judge *has* that moral belief is *not* a moral statement, any more than the statement that Euclid held a certain mathematical belief is a mathematical statement. Nor need the lawyer *be* a moral pacifist to believe that the judge is one. By contrast, the majority in *Lochner* defended a decree by appealing not only to general principles of legal duty and to statements of fact but also to Spencer's moral beliefs, while the dissenting Holmes appealed to a principle that was equally moral.

Holmes's Parochial Jurisprudence

The inconsistency between Holmes's view that a judge who defends a decree appeals only to rules of law that are generalized *prophecies* and his view that his brethren in *Lochner* appealed to Spencer's moral principle may have been due to his conflating the law as conceived by the predicting lawyer and law as conceived by the judge, but I think it may also have been due to the limitations he imposed on his legal philosophy or jurisprudence. Holmes says in "The Path of the Law" that "every effort to reduce a case to a rule is an effort of jurisprudence" and that jurisprudence follows "the existing body of dogma into its highest generalizations." But Holmes then reveals his circumscribed view of jurisprudence by adding, as I have indicated, that attempts "to analyze legal ideas have been confused by striving for a useless quintessence of all systems, instead of an accurate anatomy of one" (pp. 196–97). This claim suggests that Holmes had little interest in finding a general criterion for the concept of legally constituted authority—such as a judge—a concept he nevertheless relied on when he contrasted judicially ordered harm with harm meted out by a gunman. Had Holmes not been content to define the notion of a judge or court merely ostensively while focusing on one system of law, he might have asked what the general criterion is for being a legal authority such as a judge or court in a legal system.

If Holmes had asked this question, how would he have answered it? Would he have brushed it aside as one that does not interest bad men who pay lawyers to tell them how to avoid "the risk of coming against what is so much stronger than themselves"? I hope not, because the only reason Holmes seems to have for saying that a woman has no *legal* obligation to surrender her diamond ring to a threatening gunman is that the gunman's threatened force is not legally authorized whereas court-ordered force is. But what makes the use of public force legal? Merely its strength? Would Holmes have said that a force exerted by the public through the courts and the police is legally authoritative simply because the public force is stronger than that of a gunman? In avoiding such questions Holmes avoided saying on what grounds the ultimate legal authority in a nation rests, partly, I think, because of his concentration on what he called the anatomy of one legal system and his lack of interest in what he called the useless quintessence of all legal systems. Though sympathetic to those who do not seek essences, I do not believe that Holmes had to seek the quintessence of law in order to say what distinguished legally authorized force from that of a gunman. He might have drawn that distinction by engaging in ethical inquiry more thoroughly than he did: that is to say, he might have inquired into the moral concept of a just force as opposed to a strong force. The client and his lawyer may be content to know what a strong authority will or will not order, but a legal philosopher—even one with Holmes's empirical predilections—should be interested in more than that.

We see, then, that Holmes used a heavy dose of what he called cynical acid to wash out his interest in two fundamental philosophical questions—the role of ethical considerations in determining what a legal authority is, and the role of legal rules as opposed to generalized prophecies in the judge's thinking. He avoids the problem of legal authority because he thinks that it may lead him into ethics, and he avoids treating the difficult notion of a normative legal rule by reducing it to the notion of a generalized prophecy of what judges will in fact do. However, we have seen that his own statements in his *Lochner* dissent and elsewhere show that judges appeal to considerations of social advantage or ethics, and that the method used by judges in defending judicial decrees of obligation runs counter to the view that legal rules are merely generalized prophecies of what judges will do. We have seen that a legal rule does not say that every person of a certain kind and in a certain condition *will be decreed* by judges to have a legal duty to report for military service, for if it did, it would be false. Instead, it says that every person of a certain kind *has* a legal duty to report for military service, thereby supporting the view that a judge tries to follow legal *rules* when issuing his decrees, even though those rules may have come into existence because an earlier judge, as James said, had twisted previous law and a novel case into fresh law.

Holism, the Predicting Lawyer, and the Judge

In concluding this chapter I want to emphasize some differences between the Holmesian lawyer's defense of his prediction and the Holmesian judge's defense of his decree. When the lawyer defends his prediction of a decree to an inquisitive client, he relies on descriptive premises because he is primarily engaged in a psychological inquiry. His premises when made explicit assert that the judge will in fact assume certain legal rules, that he will in fact assume certain factual and logical beliefs, and that he in fact has certain personal traits, such as honesty and logical acuity. Therefore, when the lawyer derives a factual prediction from his premises that turns out to be false, he may in the spirit of epistemic holism return to any one of his premises to see where he went wrong, much as any scientist would in similar circumstances. By contrast, a judge who defends his decree assumes some legal rules that are not empirical statements (notwithstanding Holmes's view that those rules are generalized prophecies), empirical statements of fact, and moral beliefs that, according to Holmes, the judge may or may not articulate. Therefore, the judge typically derives a decree that is what I have called lowercase and that says "Jones had a legal obligation to report for military service." But this decree or ruling, I repeat, is not an empirical statement, whereas the conclusion of the predicting lawyer is. The lawyer's prediction will be rejected if the judge issues a decree that is different from the one the lawyer predicted, but the judge's decree will not be rejected on similar empirical grounds since that decree is not factually true or false. Furthermore, if Holmes denies that there is a Hartian statement of the form "JONES HAS A LEGAL OBLIGATION TO REPORT FOR MILITARY SERVICE," he cannot compare the judge's lowercase decree with Hart's capitalized counterpart of it to see whether they coincide. And since different judges, according to Holmes, make different moral assumptions, apply different legal rules, and are subject to all kinds of prejudice (and to bribery, as Hart notes), they issue different and even contradictory decrees about the same action.

Holmes the anti-formalist wrote: "The danger of which I speak [is] the notion that a given system, ours, for instance, can be worked out like mathematics from some general axioms of conduct. This is the natural error of the schools, but it is not confined to them. I once heard a very eminent judge say that he never let a decision go until he was absolutely sure that it was right. So judicial dissent often is blamed, as if it meant simply that one side or the other were not doing their sums right, and, if they would take more trouble, agreement inevitably would come" (p. 180). This statement suggests that in Holmes's view judicial decrees are not supported as lawyers' predictions are supported. In principle, several lawyers who are independently retained by a client to predict a decree may be expected to arrive at the same prediction, as scientists are expected to do, but we know that the same is not true of judges, especially those on the Supreme Court. And one reason is that a judge's decree is not a statement of fact that he supports on purely empirical grounds; it is made by a human being who appeals to legal rules, factual statements, and moral beliefs in a manner that does not yield uniform decrees. The judge's decree is like the weather, in which case the lawyer is like the weatherman.

In the next chapter we shall see that Quine held that the coherence theory of truth applies to ethics, claiming that we accept singular ethical conclusions because they are consequences of ethical principles, whereas the correspondence theory applies to science because scientific statements are factual and refutable on the basis of experience. And although I take issue with Quine's view of ethics for reasons that I give later, it may well be that the coherence theory applies to judicial reasoning. Indeed, Holmes might have foreseen the difficulty involved in regarding judicial decrees as empirically supported when he focused on the lawyer's prediction. He said in an 1899 address, "Law in Science and Science in Law": "The true science of the law does not consist mainly in a theological working out of dogma or a logical development as in mathematics";[13] this declaration comports well with his adopting the view of the man who thinks that the law consists of empirically supported predictions of what the courts will do in fact. Holmes added, however, that the true science of law does not consist "only in a study of it as an anthropological document from the outside". Indeed, he continues, an even more important part of the law consists in the establishment of its postulates *from within* [my emphasis] upon accurately measured social desires instead of tradition".[14] In this third section of the science of law, Holmes thinks, the judge rather than the predicting lawyer plays the leading role but, as I have argued, does *not always* arrive at decrees merely by logically deducing them from legal principles and statements of fact.

[13] Oliver Wendell Holmes, "Law in Science and Science in Law," in *Collected Legal Papers*, p. 225.
[14] Ibid., pp. 225–26.

I emphasize the phrase "not always" because I believe Holmes thought that sometimes the judge deduces his decree from a simple general principle of the form "Every person of kind K and in condition C has a legal obligation to do O" and a factual statement like "Jones is a person of kind K who is in condition C"; in other words, he seems to have thought that in some cases the judge proceeds deductively from a rule and a factual statement. But he adds quickly that "Whenever a doubtful case arises, with certain analogies on one side and other analogies on the other, . . . what really is before us is a conflict between two social desires, each of which seeks to extend its dominion over the case, and which cannot both have their way." The social question, Holmes continues, is which desire is stronger at the point of conflict; but the judicial question may be narrower, because "one or the other desire may have been expressed in previous decisions to such an extent that logic requires us to assume it to preponderate in the one before us. But if that be clearly so, the case is not a doubtful one." However, Holmes concludes this part of "Law in Science and Science in Law" by emphasizing that "where there is doubt the simple tool of logic does not suffice, and even if it is disguised and unconscious the judges are called on to exercise the sovereign prerogative of choice."[15]

Why, one may ask, is this third part of the law *scientific* from Holmes's point of view? It would seem that Holmes thinks that here the judge measures which of two competing social desires is stronger, and also thinks that the process is like measuring whether one body is heavier than another. That is why Holmes regards the judge who decides a doubtful case as an empirical scientist, just as he regards the predicting lawyer. However, Holmes does not seem to recognize here that a judge who decides a doubtful case often does *not* engage in purely scientific weighing of social desires but rather applies a moral view about which of the competing social desires *should* dominate. In other words, the judge adopts a view like that adopted by

[15] Ibid., p. 239.

the majority in *Lochner*, who, in Holmes's view, unconsciously assumed the moral principle of Spencer when making their decision.
Once we recognize this tendency of judges and see that their reasoning in doubtful cases often rests on opposing moral premises, we
may see more readily why they arrive at opposing decisions. Although they may aim at unanimous decisions, their failure to arrive
at them often derives from their adopting conflicting moral premises
about which social desire *should* prevail instead of from adopting
premises about which social desire is in fact stronger. If the judge's
task in such a case were always like that of measuring two forces with
a dynamometer, judges would always ask a question that could in
principle be answered with unanimity. But deciding whether the social desire to protect the fetus's life *should* prevail over the social
desire to protect the mother's life is very different from deciding
which desire is stronger in society. And since we are not as likely to
reach unanimity on this questions as we are when measuring the
social strength of desires, judges, being human, disagree in their decrees more than lawyers disagree in predicting those decrees.

Holmes once said that "our system of morality is a body of imper-
fect social generalizations expressed in terms of emotions," and that
"deep-seated preferences cannot be argued about—you cannot
argue a man into liking a glass of beer."[16] But he also said that to get
at the truth of a system of morality, it is useful "to omit the emotion"
and to ask ourselves what its component social generalizations are
"and how far they are confirmed by fact accurately ascertained."[17]
But can the judge establish the precedence of the desire to protect
the fetus rather than the mother by defending a social generalization
that is confirmed by fact accurately ascertained? What generalization would this be? Would it be that all or most human beings prefer
the protection of the fetus? I doubt it. Would it be that all or most
Americans have a stronger desire to protect the fetus than to protect

---

[16] Oliver Wendell Holmes, "Ideals and Doubts," in *Collected Legal Papers*, p. 306; "Natural
Law," in ibid., p. 312.
[17] Holmes, "Ideals and Doubts," p. 306.

the mother? I doubt that as well, and I doubt that Holmes could have formulated the factual social generalization he would use if he were deciding a case in which he was called upon to weigh two such opposing claims. True, Holmes said that we must distinguish two assertions, "that such and such a condition is desirable and that such and such means are appropriate to bring it about,"[18] but he never seriously addressed the ethical problem of the morally desirable, or what *should be* or *is worthy of* being desired.

What this shows again is Holmes's failure to come to grips with certain difficult problems in moral philosophy. He made us aware of such problems when he distinguished judicially authorized harm from that administered by a gunman, but he failed to clarify the notion of legal authority or that of the morally desirable because he shied away from ethics. He tried to answer "What constitutes the law?" by treating it as a question about the meaning of the word "law" but spoke sloppily about meaning. He tells us what the word "law" means while dealing with only one context of its use, but he fails to see that a judge, unlike a lawyer, does not predict a decree but issues one and therefore does not use the word "law" as the predicting lawyer does. He called legal rules generalized prophecies of decrees, failing to recognize that they formulate duties and rights and do not expressly state what past or future courts *will* say. After arguing in "The Path of the Law" that a predicting lawyer rests only on generalized prophecies of what judges will say, Holmes showed in his *Lochner* dissent that a lawyer should know something about a judge's moral views if the lawyer wishes to predict the judge's decision. And, as we have seen, he seemed to hold that a judge's moral views about the ordering of values rest on factual social generalizations.

Generally speaking, Holmes wanted to get as much empiricism into the law as possible, as we can see in his view that the lawyer predicts what the court will do, in his view that legal rules are generalized prophecies, and in his view that moral principles are general-

---

[18] Ibid.

izations that are confirmed by ascertaining facts. But laudable as his empiricism and his anti-rationalism were, they left him with problems that require more philosophical care than he devoted to them. His view of the law is often associated with pragmatism because of its preoccupation with prediction but, like many early versions of pragmatism, it suffers from not being explicitly holistic and from being insufficiently mindful of questions surrounding the word "meaning". I venture to speculate, therefore, that if Holmes had been writing about law a century later, when philosophers and philosophical lawyers were more attentive to certain views in the philosophy of language, Holmes might have accepted part, but not all, of what I have said about his view of the law.

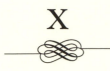

X

Holistic Pragmatism, Ethics, and Rawls's Theory of Justice

S O FAR I HAVE DISCUSSED A NUMBER OF QUES-
tions about religion, art, science, history, and
law as treated by philosophers who abandoned classical rationalism
in favor of holistic pragmatism, but I have not discussed the impact
of holism on ethical theory at length. Therefore I want to make a
case for applying holistic pragmatism to moral philosophy in a manner not favored by Quine but followed to a considerable degree by
John Rawls in his work on justice. Before doing so, however, I shall
add something to my earlier remarks on the history of applying holistic pragmatism to science in general.

As we have seen, holistic pragmatism differs from James's in a
way that Russell noted in 1908, when he said that James held in
Pragmatism that there are two kinds of truths that are not subject to
pragmatic testing, a view inconsistent with the pragmatic holism
Russell attributed to James only a year later. One of these kinds of
truth James illustrated by "1 and 1 make 2" and by "White differs
less from gray than it does from black"; he calls these "eternal
truths" that are "perceptually obvious at a glance" and in no need
of "sense-verification." The other kind of nonpragmatic truth,
James says, is in accord with "the sensible facts of experience".
When characterizing these two sorts of truths, James writes: "Between the coercions of the sensible order and those of the ideal
order, our mind is thus wedged tightly. Our ideas must agree with

realities, be such realities concrete or abstract, be they facts or be they principles". James then remarks that intellectualists—whom he also calls rationalists—"can raise no protest" to this view;[1] and they cannot, of course, because James conceded that truths in accord with relations between ideas are not abandoned on empirical grounds. Whereas in 1909 Russell said that James was a holist, or someone who thought that mathematics was part of a Duhemian conjunction that faces facts, a year earlier Russell had maintained that James exempted arithmetical truths from such a test. In 1908 Russell remarked of James's view in *Pragmatism*, "It is only when we pass beyond plain matters of fact and *a priori* truisms that the pragmatic notion of truth comes in."[2] Russell went on to say that James held that statements which are neither *a priori* nor in agreement with the sensible facts of experience are true if and only if it pays to believe them, thereby limiting the class of statements we establish pragmatically.

I shall not linger over the question of whether Russell fairly attributed this commercial theory of truth to James: enough ink has been spilled over that. However, I want to point out that while Quine later held with Tarski that mathematico-logical statements may be surrendered in the face of an adverse experience, he treated the beliefs that James said were coerced "by the sensible order" with much more respect than he accorded those that James said were coerced "by the ideal order". Quine's holism excluded "sensible truths" from the Duhemian conjunction that is tested by appeal to them, but his naturalistic epistemology, as he called it, led him to characterize them without saying that they are in accord with subjective experiences. However—and this is of most concern to me in this chapter— Quine differentiates more sharply than I do between an observation sentence like "That's a rabbit" and the sentence "That ought not to

---

[1]   William James, *Pragmatism*, [ed. Fredson Bowers and Ignas K. Skrupskelis] (Cambridge, Mass., 1975), pp. 100–102.

[2]   Bertrand Russell, *Philosophical Essays* (London, 1910), p. 134. See my *Science and Sentiment in America: Philosophical Thought from Jonathan Edwards to John Dewey* (New York, 1972), pp. 204–16.

be done" or "That's outrageous", its counterparts in my view of the confirmation of ethical beliefs. That difference between us reflects my inclination to emphasize the similarity between ethical and scientific thinking and Quine's different inclination. In order to compare my view with his, I must first say something about Quine's view of observation sentences.

Observation Sentences

Well versed as Quine was in the history of logical positivism, he contrasted his views on this matter with those debated in the Vienna Circle over what to count as observation sentences, or *Protokollsätze*. One position, he said, was that they were reports of sense impressions, a view close to that expressed by William James in *The Varieties of Religious Experience*, where he called them reports of "subjective phenomena". Quine also revealed the direct or indirect influence of James in his "Two Dogmas of Empiricism" when he wrote that man-made science is a tool "for working a manageable structure into the flux of experience".[3] "Experience" in that essay seems to refer to sensory experiences that James located in the "private breast", but Quine later dropped James's way of speaking and instead called observation sentences the public linguistic checkpoints of science, avoiding talk about sensory experiences. He labeled the old Viennese debates fruitless and turned his back on the question of whether observation sentences report sense impressions or are sentences like "Otto Neurath now sees a red cube on the table". Quine tried "to view the matter unreservedly in the context of the external world" by eschewing talk about experiences within the mind,[4] and therefore presented a view of observation sentences that in one respect resem-

---

[3] W. V. Quine, "Two Dogmas of Empiricism," in *From a Logical Point of View: Nine Logico-Philosophical Essays* (Cambridge, Mass., 1953), p. 44.

[4] W. V. Quine, "Epistemology Naturalized," in *Ontological Relativity and Other Essays* (New York, 1969), p. 85.

bled his view that clear synonymy-statements should be behavioristic and empirical, Tarski's view that holism is a descriptive psychological theory about what we are prepared to surrender in the face of adverse experience, and Goodman's onetime view that the synonym of a term is the expression that we think is most likely to have the same extension as that term. Such views avoided referring to entities such as meanings, essences, attributes, or concepts in the mind, and in a similar spirit Quine avoided referring to private subjective experiences or sense-data when considering observation sentences. This approach survived Quine's rejection of phenomenalism and the positivistic distinction between analytic and synthetic statements; and so he remained an empiricist about science insofar as he held that it is anchored by observation sentences that he separated from the conjunction of scientific sentences that they anchor, just as a real anchor is separated from a ship though connected to it. As a behavioristic epistemologist, Quine held that dispositions to assent to or to dissent from observation sentences are manifested in linguistic responses to the external world that are in closest causal proximity to our sensory receptors. Here especially Quine's talk reminds one of James's talk about coercions of the sensible order, since Quine holds that our verdicts about observation sentences are virtually forced on us under certain circumstances.

Quine's view of observation sentences also reminds one of Locke's characterization of self-evident truths as propositions that "are generally assented to as soon as proposed, and the terms they are proposed in understood." Locke adds that "all men, even children, as soon as they hear and understand the terms, assent to these propositions,"[5] and the especially relevant feature of a Lockeian self-evident truth when compared with Quine's observation sentence is that it is generally assented to *as soon as proposed*. Lockeian assent that comes simultaneously with understanding is a forerunner of Quine's notion of assent to "That's a rabbit" as a quick linguistic

[5] John Locke, *An Essay Concerning Human Understanding*, edited by Peter H. Nidditch (Oxford, 1975), book II, chap. I, sec. 17 (p. 56).

response to external stimuli on the part of witnesses who understand the language; according to Quine, all speakers who understand the language are disposed to return the same verdict on an observation sentence when given the same concurrent stimulation. Upon having their nerve endings stimulated, they tend quickly to assent to or dissent from "That's a rabbit" if they understand that sentence. Thus their verdict does not hinge on what Quine calls collateral information that would in his view taint the observationality of the sentence if it played a part in bringing about the verdict.

I turn now to my disagreement with Quine about ethics. Unlike him, I think that a conjunction containing a normative ethical principle and a descriptive statement may be viewed in a holistic fashion *and* tested empirically.[6] It is obvious that it can be viewed in this way if we accept a reductionist form of utilitarianism according to which all ethical statements are deemed synonymous with statements of descriptive behavioral science, but my approach is different. Avoiding the view that ethical sentences are synonymous with sociological or psychological sentences, and being impressed by the failure of reductive phenomenalism as well as the power of holism to bridge the traditional epistemic gap created by the distinction between the analytic and the synthetic, I propose a nonreductive version of holism in order to bridge the gap between the moral and the descriptive much as Tarski and Quine had bridged that between logic and physics. In earlier writings in which he developed his use of Duhem's approach, Quine distinguished (a) the scientific thinker, (b) the body of science that such a thinker uses as a tool for organizing sensory experiences, and (c) those sensory experiences themselves. Analogously, when I deal with moral belief, I distinguish (a′) the moral thinker; (b′) the conjunction of logical, descriptive, *and*

---

[6] I advocate a form of this view of ethics in *Toward Reunion in Philosophy* (Cambridge, Mass., 1956), in *What Is and What Ought to Be Done: An Essay on Ethics and Epistemology* (New York, 1981), and in *The Question of Free Will: A Holistic View* (Princeton, 1993). According to Hilary Putnam, Peirce advocated a similar view; see Putnam's "Comments" in C. S. Peirce, *Reasoning and the Logic of Things*, ed. K. L. Ketner (Cambridge, Mass., 1992), p. 55. Also see Peirce's remarks on sentiment, p. 111.

moral beliefs he uses as a tool for organizing the flux of sensory experiences *and* feelings of moral obligation; and (c′) those sensory experiences and feelings themselves. In enlarging the tool of the moral thinker and the pool of that thinker's experiences I follow James's view in *Pragmatism*, where he speaks of "the flux of our sensations and emotions as they pass."[7]

In accordance with this approach, I ask the reader to suppose that the following argument is presented by a moral critic of abortion with whom a mother disagrees:

1. Every human being who kills another human being does something that ought not to be done.
2. The mother killed a fetus in her womb.
3. Every live fetus is a human being.

Therefore,

4. The mother killed a human being.

Therefore,

5. The mother did something that ought not to be done.

Next I ask the reader to imagine that the mother did not feel morally obligated *not* to have done what she did; indeed, she felt obligated—that is, felt that she ought—to have done it. She therefore denies statement (5), and this denial leads her to reject the moral principle (1) among the premises and to view the whole situation differently. She may argue as follows:

6. Every mother who is sane, who is in very poor physical health, who carries an unhealthy fetus, and who has been incestuously raped, ought to kill the fetus.
7. I was in very poor physical health.
8. I was carrying an unhealthy fetus.

[7] James, *Pragmatism*, p. 93.

9. I was incestuously raped.

10. I was sane.

Therefore,

11. I had an obligation to kill the fetus.

The next step in the mother's argument is to say that she *felt* obligated to kill the fetus. This step she defends by saying that any sane person who *has* an obligation to do something will normally feel obligated to do it. This is the counterpart of maintaining with Peirce (and Dewey, I think) that if a table is *really* brown, it will *look* brown to a person of normal vision.

In my view, the mother's dissent from (5) is similar to that of a physicist who has a sensory experience that runs counter to one predicted by a theory; the physicist has what Quine once called a recalcitrant sensory experience, and I say that the mother has a recalcitrant feeling of disobligation when denying (5). I also say that she has a supportive feeling of obligation when she confirms (11) and the conjunction leading to it. Believing that after denying (5) the mother may deny the conjunction that logically implies it, I maintain that the mother may amend or surrender an ethical principle such as (1), or she may deny a descriptive statement among the premises that jointly lead to the singular ethical conclusion—for example, statement (3) that every live fetus is a human being. A logical statement is rarely recanted in the light of a recalcitrant experience, whether sensory or emotional, just as a descriptive statement in a moral argument is rarely recanted after we have such an experience; but I think that we sometimes reject or alter a descriptive statement in response to an adverse moral feeling, as when some participants in the debate over abortion deny that a fetus is a human being in order to accommodate their feeling that it ought to be or may be killed.

Because I assign this role to feeling morally obligated or feeling that one has a moral right, I do not agree with Quine that whereas we can test a prediction in physics against the independent course of observable nature, we can judge the morality of an act only by our moral standards or principles themselves. For this reason, as I indicate in the previous chapter, I disagree with Quine's view that while science "thanks to its links with observation, retains some title to a correspondence theory of truth, a coherence theory is evidently the lot of ethics".[8] In my view, a coherence theory is not the lot of ethics, for if descriptive science retains some title to a correspondence theory of truth "thanks to its link with observation", then ethics retains some title to a correspondence theory of truth thanks to its links with *sensory observation and a feeling of obligation*. Like Quine, I think that ethics has a foothold in the observable act which corresponds to descriptive science's foothold in the predictable observable event, but I also think that just as we test conjunctions of descriptive science by appealing to what is sensed, we test systems of ethical thinking such as the conjunction of statements (6) through (11) above by appealing to what is sensed *and* what is felt as obligatory. Because the feeling of obligation plays the part I assign to it, I do not think that ethics is doomed to accepting the coherence theory of truth that Quine associates with it. Ethics is also anchored in experience when that includes feelings of obligation.

To this argument Quine responds by recalling that he has become a naturalistic epistemologist who eschews talk about experiences and who takes sentences as the checkpoints of science.[9] He says that an observation sentence is what he calls an occasion sentence—true on some occasions, false on others—that elicits the same verdict from all witnesses who know the language; and despite some later conciliatory remarks about how being observational is a matter of degree, he seems to deny that the occasion sentence "That's outrageous", when uttered by a man who sees someone beating a handicapped

---

[8] W. V. Quine, "On the Nature of Moral Values," in *Theories and Things* (Cambridge, Mass., 1981), p. 64.

[9] W. V. Quine, "Reply to Morton White," in *The Philosophy of W. V. Quine*, ed. Lewis Edwin Hahn and Paul Arthur Schilpp, 2nd ed. (Chicago, 1998), pp. 663–65.

person, is an observation sentence. Adopting for the sake of argument what he calls a best-case but unrealistic assumption that everyone in our linguistic community (save perhaps the wrongdoer) is disposed to assent to "That's outrageous" upon witnessing that act, Quine says that even if everyone were so disposed, "That's outrageous" would not count as an observation sentence for him. Why? Because, Quine says as he levels what he regards as a decisive objection to my view, "That's outrageous" applies not only to his illustrative act of cripple beating but also to acts whose outrageousness depends on collateral information that is seldom widely shared. By contrast, the sentence "It's raining" almost never hinges on information not shared by present witnesses and "That's a rabbit" does so only seldom. Both of these sentences qualify as observational for Quine because being observational is "a status that is somewhat a matter of degree."[10] He also says that "He's a bachelor" is at the other end of the scale from "It's raining", because verdicts on "He's a bachelor" depend on information that is seldom widely shared. However, Quine adds, in what may be a concession to my view, that on this scale "That's outrageous" lies between "That's a rabbit" and "He's a bachelor".

In response, I am willing to speak of sentences rather than experiences as checkpoints, and therefore make my point within Quine's behavioristic framework. I would first remark that if being a scientific discipline depends on having observational checkpoints like "It's raining", and if being an observational sentence is somewhat a matter of degree, then the epistemic difference between ethics and science, like the difference between "That's outrageous" and "It's raining", is somewhat a matter of degree. Granting that ethics may be called a soft science whereas physics is a hard science,[11] I think the difference between soft and hard is obviously one of degree. Indeed, Quine's epistemology is on his own view soft inasmuch as

---

[10] Ibid., p. 664.

[11] On soft and hard sciences, see W. V. Quine, *From Stimulus to Science* (Cambridge, Mass., 1995), p. 49.

it is a branch of psychology, which he calls one of the softer sciences along with economics, sociology, and history. In these sciences, he says, checkpoints or observation sentences are sparser and sparser, to the point that their absence becomes rather the rule than the exception. It would appear, then, that ethics is not in completely unscientific company from his point of view, even though it is not as hard as physics; and, ironically, it may not be softer than the epistemological science in which Quine calls it soft. Indeed, the sparsity of observation sentences in psychology that Quine mentions is illustrated by the difficulty he might have in marshaling many observation sentences to support his belief that "That's a rabbit" is an observation sentence. For Quine's epistemological sentence " 'That's a rabbit' is an observation sentence" is of course different from the sentence "That's a rabbit" in his book, and it might be hard to present many observation sentences that serve as checkpoints for the holistic conjunction of which Quine's epistemological sentence is a component—in which case Quine's epistemological pot may be calling my ethical kettle black.

I now want to go beyond what may be regarded as an *ad hominem* argument and show that Quine's first arrow against my view—the one involving his best-case assumption—can be dodged and that the sentence "That's outrageous" or the sentence "That ought not to be done" is observational enough on his scale of observationality to call into question his view that we can judge the morality of an act only by our moral principles and that a coherence theory of truth is the lot of ethics. To that end, I shall argue that Quine's best-case "unrealistic" assumption is less unrealistic than he supposes. Quine says that a sentence such as "That's an elephant" is observational if and only if every fluent speaker of English is disposed to give a verdict on it quickly without any collateral information save that which is involved in understanding this sentence. But when faced with the fact that veteran experimental physicists quickly and jointly assent to "That's a condenser" or "That's an X-ray tube", Quine allows that the condition of being a fluent speaker of English may be replaced by that of being a fluent speaker of the language of those physicists, thereby permitting "That's a condenser" to be observational in that smaller community. However, Quine goes on to say that we can "always get an absolute standard by taking in all speakers of the language, or most", remarking that he adds the qualification "or most" to allow for "occasional deviants such as the insane or the blind".[12] By contrast, however, when Quine formulates his best-case but allegedly unrealistic assumption about "That's outrageous", the stronger condition he imposes is that "*all* [my emphasis] speakers [be] disposed to assent to 'That's outrageous' on seeing a man beat a cripple",[13] not most speakers. But is it unrealistic to say that *most* speakers in my community and Quine's are disposed to assent to "That's outrageous" under those circumstances? Since I believe most speakers in Quine's and my linguistic community are so disposed, I believe the assumption *is* realistic if we are as liberal in our standards of observationality as Quine is when he relies on the responses of *most* speakers to "That's a rabbit" or, of speakers in his community of veteran physicists, to "That's a condenser". If we weaken the requirement for observationality in this way, I submit that Quine's best-case assumption is not all that unrealistic.

Now I come to what I call Quine's second arrow against my view. He says that even if his best-case scenario involving "That's outrageous" were to be realized—even if all fluent speakers of the language were to declare it true—a second problem would arise for my view. We have seen that for Quine the sentence "That's outrageous" applies to acts other than his illustrative act of cripple beating because it applies to acts "whose outrageousness hinges on collateral information not in general shared by all witnesses of the acts."[14] So let us assume that Pecksniff applies the sentence "That's outrageous" to acts other than the act of cripple beating that Quine and I witness and call outrageous because Pecksniff has information about

[12] Quine, "Epistemology Naturalized," p. 88 n. 7.
[13] Quine, "Reply to Morton White," p. 664.
[14] Ibid.

those acts that we do not have. We must remember that according to Quine, a sentence is an observation sentence *if and only if all* speakers who understand it are disposed to assent to or dissent from it upon concurrent stimulation without collateral information. Therefore "That's outrageous" is not an observation sentence for Quine, because Pecksniff for one utters it about an act on the basis of information about the act that Quine and I do not have, information that is not widely shared.

To this I reply that Quine's second arrow may just as well be directed against the observationality of "That's green". Suppose Helmholtz uttered this sentence while pointing to a leaf and with the agreement of all other eyewitnesses of the leaf's color. Now suppose Ångström and his friends instead look at a leaf through optical instruments and that the Ångströmites are disposed to say "That's green" in unison as soon as their instruments register that the light coming from the leaf has a wavelength of 5,461 angstrom units, which they know to be the wavelength of green. In that case, Ångström and friends would be disposed to assent to "That's green" on the basis of information that Helmholtz and friends do not have; therefore Quine's second arrow may as legitimately be directed at the observationality of the sentence "That's green" as it is directed by him at the observationality of "That's outrageous". After all, the Ångströmites are disposed to apply "true" to that sentence because they have collateral information that the Helmholtzians do not have. And if Quine were to say that the Ångströmites are not direct eyewitnesses of the leaf and that their disposition to affirm "That's green" is collateral because they assume certain physical laws governing their instrument, one might ask Quine how he regards the verdicts of witnesses who look through telescopes or eyeglasses. Do they utter them on the basis of collateral information that depends on the optics of lenses or not?

I want now to say something related about Quine's supplementary defense of his view when he distinguishes between sensation and emotion. He says that "sensation is nicely coordinated with concurrent, publicly accessible stimulation. Impacts on a certain range of surface receptors produce the sensation, and conversely, apart from occasional illusion, the sensation occurs only when thus produced".[15] But note Quine's qualification "apart from occasional illusion". Veteran hunters who worry about illusions do not give quick assent to "That's an elephant" if and only if their surface receptors are hit in a certain way. They do not assent to it quickly because they have had hallucinatory experiences that they do not distinguish from sensations they have while seeing elephants—experiences they have when their receptors are stimulated not by rays coming from an elephant but rather as a result of having seizures of delirium tremens. Quine disregards such illusions when characterizing sensation; and once he has brushed them aside as rare, he can of course say that we usually have a sensation just in case our receptors are bombarded in a certain way, and also deny that we usually have an emotion of outrage just in case our receptors are bombarded in a certain way. Why? Because he thinks human beings have an emotion like outrage as a consequence of having collateral information about an act and therefore by a causal route that differs from direct bombardment of their receptors. Notice, however, that if we take into account hallucinations, we may say that assent to "That's an elephant" is caused not only by irradiation of our sensory receptors but also by attacks of delirium tremens when we are not looking at elephants. This duality of the causes of our sensations is paralleled by the fact that our emotions are caused by the direct stimulation of an act that elicits quick assent to "That's outrageous" *and* by having information about the act that Pecksniff has but Quine does not have. Having an attack of delirium tremens and being stimulated by rays of light *both* cause hunters to say "That's an elephant" is true. To make the situations more similar, suppose that several hallucinating drunks are disposed to apply "true" to "That's an elephant" simultaneously, and that several sober individuals who have their receptors

---

[15] Ibid.

bombarded in the Quinian way are disposed to apply "true" to the same sentence.

Underlying Quine's inclination to distinguish as he does between "That's outrageous" and "That's a rabbit" is his belief that his observation sentences are more anchor-like than my feeling sentences are because "That's a rabbit" is more likely than "That's outrageous" to be called true or false without depending on collateral information that is inside what he calls the ship of science. In other words, Quine's observation sentences are usually not dependent on accepting other statements in the Duhemian conjunction to be tested, whereas my feeling sentences often are. But I emphasize that this is a difference of degree, as I think Quine may admit. How big a difference of degree, I do not know, but I repeat that Quine's observation sentences are *understood* by witnesses, and their understanding of such sentences may, he says, depend on information contained in the Duhemian conjunction or scientific ship that observation sentences collectively anchor. Because Quine's anchor sentences are not *completely* separable from sentences inside his ship, it may be argued that this overlap taints the observationality of "That's a rabbit" just as Pecksniff's collateral information taints the observationality of "That's outrageous". In any case, I think Nelson Goodman has argued persuasively—and, I would add, holistically—that because so-called observation sentences are often contingent on the acceptance of other beliefs in what I have been calling a Duhemian conjunction, they are not so certain as to be unsurrenderable by contrast to sentences in the Duhemian conjunction itself. I turn now to Goodman's views on their surrenderability and then argue that feeling sentences, like Goodman's observation sentences, may be surrendered—this in the interest of showing that natural science and ethics are not as different as Quine may think they are.

Goodman says that a judgment he had made a few moments earlier that a reddish patch occupied the center of his visual field at that moment will be dropped by him if it conflicts with other judgments having a combined stronger claim to preservation. For example, if he had judged that the patch occupying the same region an instant later was bluish, and also that the apparent color of the patch was constant over the brief period covering the two instants, he would have to drop one of the three judgments (if he accepted a certain logical principle); and he might be led to drop the judgment that the patch was reddish. He says that he might conclude that the patch could not have been reddish after all, since he was looking at a blue jay in sunlight with his eyes functioning normally. In other words, his first observation sentence that the patch was reddish was withdrawn by him later because the statement that he was looking at a blue jay in the sunlight with his eyes functioning normally had a stronger claim to preservation.[16] And what I maintain is that if the mother I mentioned were persuaded by the argument from (1), (2), (3), and (4) to say that (5) is true and that she felt obligated to kill her fetus, she would reject an opposing feeling sentence that she might have accepted earlier.

Here some more general observations about the issue between Quine and me would be useful. Quine seeks to formulate a criterion for identifying an observation sentence so that he can characterize what *he* calls cognitive or scientific judgment by contrast to moral judgment, but there is, of course, a respectable tradition in philosophy according to which moral judgment *and* physical judgment are both cognitive. I associate myself with that tradition and therefore do not think that its adherents can be dismissed as legalistic quibblers when they resist including physical thinking as cognitive while excluding ethical thinking. What separates Quine and me on this issue is not his behaviorism but his selective behaviorism, which is motivated by his initial philosophical inclination to regard knowledge more narrowly than I do and which impels him to build epistemic walls between science and ethics that I decline to build or buttress. It has sometimes seemed to me that if Quine were to discover that a proposed criterion for being cognitive *did* apply to ethical

---

[16] Nelson Goodman, "Sense and Certainty," in *Problems and Projects* (New York, 1992), pp. 60–61.

statements, he might count that as an argument *against* the criterion, whereas I am inclined to say that a criterion for being cognitive which leads to the conclusion that ethical statements are *not* cognitive is defective for that very reason. After all, most of us say that we believe, and some of us say we know, that ethical statements are true. That is one reason why I have argued that they are accepted as elements of a Duhemian conjunction which is anchored in sensory experience *and* emotional experience, and that in ethics we use a Duhemian conjunction to work a manageable structure into the flux of sensations *and* feelings of obligation.

The view I have defended is in a certain respect like one that Quine defended when he argued that ontological statements are as scientific as physical statements. Some logical empiricists had held that any philosophical theory which declared ontological statements to be scientific or cognitive was unacceptable on that very account; they advocated a so-called empiricist criterion of meaning because they regarded metaphysical speculation as cognitively meaningless and therefore wanted to show that being scientific and being onto-logico-metaphysical are mutually exclusive, just as Quine wants to show that being scientific and being ethical are. My own inclination concerning ethics is to continue on a path like the one that Quine took when he questioned the epistemic separation of science and ontology, and that is why I do not share his inclination to distinguish between the cognitive and the moral by opening doors to "That's a rabbit" which he closes to "That ought to be done", "That ought not to be done", and "That's outrageous". I am thus encouraged by his remark that the distinction between "It's raining" and "That's outrageous" is somewhat a matter of degree and by his willingness to put the latter sentence between "He's a bachelor" and "That's a rabbit" on his scale of observationality. For that reason, I do not agree with his view that we can judge the moral obligatoriness of an act *only* by our moral principles themselves, since such a position lends support to the view that our ethical principles are self-evident guarantors of singular moral judgments that have no anchor in our feelings. I avoid that view by anchoring a conjunction of moral beliefs and descriptive beliefs in a combination of Quine's observation sentences and sentences such as "That's outrageous"; and I avoid the view that a coherence theory is the lot of ethics by saying that experience includes feelings of obligation as well as sensory experiences. However, I do not believe that observation sentences as I conceive them form an absolutely inalterable anchor, since I think that a sentence reporting a feeling of obligation may be rejected under certain circumstances. Neither reports of feelings of obligation nor moral principles are immutable. Therefore, when our conjunction of logical sentences, moral sentences, and descriptive sentences comes into conflict with an observation sentence as I conceive it, we may reject or revise the conjunction or we may continue to hold on to the conjunction and repudiate the observation sentence that conflicts with it.

I have occasionally called myself a methodological monist because I believe that we test both physical and moral beliefs by checking Duhemian conjunctions against a pool of experiences—in the former case a pool consisting wholly of sensory experiences, and in the latter a pool composed of sensory experiences and feelings of obligation. I decline to say with James that there are sentences which can be seen to be unsurrenderable merely by inspecting entities in what James called an ideal order, and I decline to say with him that observation sentences are seen to be true merely by noting "the sensible facts of experience" and concluding on the basis of such noting that they can never be surrendered. In the early pages of this chapter and in chapter 5 we saw that James held that our mind is wedged tightly between the coercions of the sensible order and those of the ideal order, and that Russell inferred from this that it is only when we pass beyond truths about plain matters of fact and *a priori* truisms that we reach surrenderable statements. However, I expand James's wedged-in middle class and assert that some logical statements, some of James's *a priori* statements, some of Kant's moral principles, some of Quine's observation sentences, and some of my feeling sentences are surrenderable. We may treat statements of any kind with great respect, but that is no guarantee that we will always respect them or kindred statements when trouble arises in a system in which they play a part.

Rawls and Holistic Pragmatism

In *A Theory of Justice* John Rawls advances a view I agree with when he speaks of what he calls reflective equilibrium. He cites Goodman's statement in *Fact, Fiction, and Forecast* (1955) that rules of inference and particular inferences are justified by being brought into agreement with each other, and that in the process of justification we make mutual adjustments between rules and actual inferences.[17] Rawls also cites with approval Goodman's denial that the rules of deductive or inductive inference follow exclusively from self-evident axioms,[18] Quine's similar views in *Word and Object*, and my effort in *Toward Reunion in Philosophy* to treat moral thought in a holistic or a corporatistic manner (p. 579). When commenting critically in sections 6 and 87 of *A Theory of Justice* on how other philosophers commonly try to justify ethical theories, Rawls says they often try to find self-evident principles from which a sufficient body of standards and principles can be derived to account for what Rawls calls our considered moral judgments. This view of justification he calls Cartesian, for it says that first principles can be seen as true, even necessarily true, and it holds that such truth or necessity will be transferable from premises to conclusion. A second approach that Rawls rejects is what may be called reductive naturalism. Reductive naturalists, he says, try to analyze or define moral concepts in terms of nonmoral

[17] John Rawls, *A Theory of Justice* (Cambridge, Mass., 1971), p. 20; this edition is hereafter cited parenthetically in the text. For an illuminating account of the use of holism by Husserl, Quine, Goodman, Rawls, and myself, and especially Husserl, see Dagfinn Føllesdal, "Husserl on Evidence and Justification," in *Edmund Husserl and the Phenomenological Tradition: Essays in Phenomenology*, ed. Robert Sokolowski (Washington, D.C., 1988), pp. 107–39.

[18] Nelson Goodman, *Fact, Fiction, and Forecast*, 2nd ed. (Indianapolis, 1965), pp. 64–65.

ones and then claim to show that affirmed moral statements, when translated by the use of such definitions, are true. Rawls accepts neither of these methods of justification. Concerning the Cartesian method he rightly points out that there are obstacles to regarding the premises as necessary truths or even to explaining what is meant by this. And concerning reductive naturalism he rightly points out that it rests on definitions or analyses that presuppose our having a clear theory of meaning which, he says, seems to be lacking.

For this reason, according to Rawls, we would do better to regard a moral theory as we would regard any other theory, leaving questions of the meaning of "good" and "right" aside and proceeding to develop a full-scale substantive theory of justice. For Rawls, as I understand him, such a theory presupposes not only logic and mathematics but also truths in economics and psychology, and he thinks the various parts of his theory make up a unified whole by supporting one another in a manner that is in accord with holistic pragmatism. Rawls says that at the top of his theory there are principles of presupposed disciplines and principles that are specific to the theory itself; at the bottom there are anchoring statements that serve as confirmatory checkpoints. However, we may note a difference between the theory Rawls defends and simpler theories that serve as illustrations in primarily epistemological discussions. At the beginning of this chapter, when I laid bare the structure of a miniature moral theory, I presented several premises and a logically deduced conclusion. Pointing out that a moral sentence may serve as a checkpoint of a moral-cum-descriptive conjunction, I said that my illustrative argument contained an unspoken logical truth, a moral principle, and factual statements in the Duhemian conjunction tested. By contrast, Rawls does not talk very much about sensory reports or reports of feelings of obligation, even though I think he might say that his theory is ultimately supported by them. Instead he operates as a philosophically oriented scientist would, building a moral theory and making epistemological comments on them without trying to anchor his theory in occasional sentences.

Rawls traces his substantive moral theory back to the theory of social contract espoused by Locke, Rousseau, and Kant and contrasts it with that of the utilitarians, so one may think of him as holding that his theory is more successful than utilitarianism at accounting for what may be called the moral phenomena; but instead of speaking of observation sentences and feeling sentences as checkpoints, he says that what he calls "considered judgments" confirm the theory he espouses. At the opposite end from his considered judgments are the fundamental principles of his theory; so, in order to understand his method, we must understand his manner of fixing on his fundamental principles, his view of a considered judgment, and his view of how these principles and considered judgments are related when they are in what he calls reflective equilibrium.

We may think of Rawls's fundamental principles of justice as components of a Duhemian conjunction that differ from what he calls confirmatory considered judgments. He characterizes these fundamental principles by means of a criterion that in a certain respect resembles one that Quine uses in characterizing observation sentences. Quine, as we have seen, identifies his observation sentences as those which fluent speakers of the language are disposed to accept or reject when stimulated in a certain way, whereas Rawls identifies his fundamental principles of justice by saying that they would be accepted by persons of a certain kind who are in a certain condition or state. Their defining feature is not the Lockeian one of being accepted very quickly by those who understand their component terms. Instead Rawls holds that fundamental principles are those that *would be* accepted by free and rational persons in what he calls an initial position of equality that defines the fundamental terms of their association without any reference to speed of acceptance or self-evidence. They are also principles that regulate all further agreements, specifying the kind of social cooperation that can be entered into and the forms of government that can be established (p. 11). The initial position of free and rational persons who accept Rawls's fundamental principles is such that none of them "knows his place in society, his class position or social status, . . . his fortune in the distribution of natural assets and liabilities, his intelligence", or his strength; they do not even know "their conception of the good or their special psychological propensities". According to Rawls, the fundamental principles of justice are collectively chosen in one joint act behind what he calls "a veil of ignorance" (p. 12). These principles, he says, "when conjoined to our beliefs and knowledge of the circumstances" would lead us to the "everyday" moral judgments we would make "were we to apply these principles conscientiously and intelligently" (p. 46). That is why I think Rawls may regard his fundamental principles as components of a Duhemian conjunction that leads by logic to considered moral judgments which support the conjunction from the bottom up. However, he adds that "we may want to change our present considered judgments once their regulative principles are brought to light" (p. 49); and so, in deference to those principles, we may withdraw or revise a considered judgment. Those regulative principles may also be withdrawn or revised in deference to considered judgments, and thus we may move back and forth from the former to the latter.

The underlying epistemological message is that the moralist, like the physicist in my opinion, may shuttle back and forth from fundamental principles to considered judgments in order to reach epistemic balance. Rawls says that the balancing in which the moral philosopher engages is more like that of the student of valid inference or the linguistic student of grammaticalness than that of the physicist, but I am inclined to say that the physicist balances the claim of theory and that of observation in a similar way. The natural scientist does not *always* defer to observation rather than to fundamental theory when they clash, and the moral philosopher does not always defer to fundamental principles rather than to considered judgments when *they* clash. The logician does not always defer more to theoretically accepted principles of inference than to actual inferences that scientists or ordinary people make. Clashes between principle and considered judgment are often resolved by a compromise, but I do not think that one side *always* gets the shorter end of the stick. Therefore, we should not view the resolution of such a conflict as do classical rationalists, for they seem to say that the palm should *always* go to fundamental principles that are called analytic, synthetic *a priori*, or self-evident. Nor should we say that the palm should *always* go to so-called considered moral judgments or to observation sentences when there is a crisis, though I agree with Quine that we usually favor observation over theory when they clash.

Kant and Holistic Pragmatism

With the above observations in mind I turn to Rawls's conception of the relation between his holism and his acceptance of the Kantian moral principle that one should never treat a person as a means only. It is often said that Kantian absolutism—the idea that moral principles admit of no qualification—is inextricably bound up with Kant's belief that such moral principles are necessary, synthetic, or *a priori*. However, Rawls disclaims such a philosophical view of moral principles while accepting the Kantian principle. That principle was once challenged by Justice Holmes,[19] who said that if we want conscripts in war—Holmes was a veteran of the Civil War—we march them up to the front with bayonets in their rear to die for a cause in which they may not believe. Moreover, we treat the enemy as an obstacle to be abolished. Holmes added that he felt no pangs of conscience over such treatment of conscripts and the enemy, and that he was reluctant to accept a moral theory that seemed to be contradicted by practices of which he approved. How would Rawls respond to this protest against the Kantian principle in question? Since he thinks that principle is not a necessary truth but part of a Duhemian conjunction that is tested by seeing whether it is confirmed by the considered judgments of rational persons, how would

---

[19] Oliver Wendell Holmes, "Ideals and Doubts," in *Collected Legal Papers* (New York, 1920), pp. 304–6.

Rawls deal with Holmes's objection? In responding to it Rawls could revise or reject the Kantian principle, for I presume that in his view no moral principle is immune to the challenge of an adverse considered judgment; or he might alter another part of the Duhemian conjunction; or he might deny Holmes's judgment or say it was not considered; or, as we shall see, he might resolve to hold on to the Kantian principle, come what may.

In an essay of 1891, "The Moral Philosopher and the Moral Life," William James wrote that "ethical science is just like physical science, and instead of being deducible all at once from abstract principles, must simply bide its time, and be ready to revise its conclusions from day to day". He also stated that the presumption is that "vulgarly accepted opinions are true, and the right casuistic order that which public opinion believes in"; but he believed, as Nietzsche did, that "every now and then, . . . some one is born with the right to be original, and his revolutionary thought or action may bear prosperous fruit. He may replace old 'laws of nature' by better ones; he may, by breaking old moral rules in a certain place, bring in a total condition of things more ideal than would have followed had the rules been kept." In this spirit James criticized "the dogmatic temper which, by absolute distinctions and unconditional 'thou shalt nots,' changes a growing, elastic, and continuous life into a superstitious system of relics and dead bones". The highest ethical life, James went on to say, "consists at all times in the breaking of rules which have grown too narrow for the actual case", and he advised moralists to respect commonly accepted moral opinions but not slavishly; to respect some considered judgments but not others; and to be wary of unconditional "thou shalt nots".[20]

Like James, I am wary of unconditional "thou shalt nots", but I don't think that the Kantian moral principle or any other may be rejected merely on the basis of such general wariness. Nor do I think that the epistemology of holistic pragmatism implies that Kant's

---

[20] William James, "The Moral Philosopher and the Moral Life," in *The Will to Believe and Other Essays in Popular Philosophy* (New York, 1898), pp. 208–9.

principle must be rejected—but it does imply that the principle is not to be accepted on grounds such as those adduced by Kant when he called it *a priori* and apodictic. Moreover, holistic pragmatism does not automatically reject all truths of logic when it says that some *may be* denied if the Duhemian conjunction of which they are components fails to organize experience successfully, and it treats hallowed principles of morality similarly. However, holistic pragmatism says that acceptance of such principles is *epistemically* conditioned on their being parts of a system that organizes a pool of experiences and feelings of obligation in a simple way that respects previously held beliefs, and with this Rawls seems to agree. Holistic pragmatism says nothing about how complicated the subject term of moral principles should be—that, for example, they should unconditionally forbid lies rather than forbid lies of a certain kind.

We know, however, that like Kant some moral philosophers are not inclined to agree that their principles are modifiable in response to their feelings of obligation or disobligation, whereas a scientist who is rebuffed by empirical evidence when he says that all bodies fall $16t^2$ feet in t seconds does not hesitate to modify his principle by saying that all *terrestrial bodies fall in a vacuum* in that way; many moral philosophers flinch from modifying their principles on analogous grounds. We know that Kant himself regarded his moral principles as *a priori* and necessary,[21] but a holistic pragmatist, such as I

---

[21] But see Kant's treatment of what he regarded as two legal exceptions to the *ius talionis*: a mother's killing of an illegitimate child and a soldier's killing another in a duel (*The Metaphysics of Morals*, trans. and ed. Mary Gregor [Cambridge, 1996], pp. 108–9). I am indebted to Professor Béatrice Longuenesse for helping me recall the exact place of this passage. The act of a mother who kills her illegitimate child, Kant says, is not legally punishable by death because "a child that comes into the world apart from marriage is born outside the law (for the law is marriage) and therefore outside the protection of the law. It has, as it were, stolen into the commonwealth (like contraband merchandise), so that the commonwealth can ignore its existence (since it was not right that it should have come to exist in this way), and can therefore also ignore its annihilation." Here, I would say, Kant allows his different feelings about mothers and illegitimate children to support a denial of a *legal* right to kill the mother while defending a *moral* right to do so. He masks the emotional basis of his view with his casuistical metaphor about the baby's stealing into the commonwealth and being contraband. Indeed, he goes *beyond* treating the baby as a means when he says that the commonwealth can ignore its existence and therefore refuse to apply the *ius talionis* to its mother.

take Rawls to be, is prepared to revise them as a physicist revises hers, and like James he is theoretically prepared to surrender a moral principle like Kant's when faced by objections like that of Holmes. A holistic pragmatist is capable of dealing with Holmes's objection by revising Kant's principle, by rejecting it, or by holding on to it no matter what the moral feelings or the considered judgments of a person such as Holmes might be. However, to reject the epistemology of holistic pragmatism because one moral principle does not pass muster before it would be like rejecting it because one physical theory does not pass muster before it. And while I admit that a belief *within* morals or science might lead one to revise or abandon holistic pragmatism, I confess that I would not abandon it because it could not accommodate Kant's principle. This, of course, raises the question of how the epistemology of holistic pragmatism is supported, a subject to which I turn in my final chapter.

XI

Philosophy as Philosophy of Culture

THE EPISTEMOLOGIST WHO ACCEPTS HOLISTIC pragmatism may initially defend it by empirically observing the behavior of scientists, but he may later come to regard it as a rule rather than a descriptive statement. When supporting it empirically, he may treat it as an experimenter treats the statement "All gases expand in accordance with Boyle's Law"—that is, by deducing consequences from "All scientists test their hypotheses in accordance with holistic pragmatism" in order to see whether it is confirmed or disconfirmed by experience of how scientists do their testing. In that case, when faced with a critic's putative counterexample to his view, the holistic pragmatist might think he has two disastrous alternatives: give up the logical principles assumed in testing holistic pragmatism or give up the thesis of holistic pragmatism itself, for his critic uses both in trying to refute his doctrine by means of the hypothetico-deductive method. His critic says that if in fact all scientists test hypotheses in accordance with holistic pragmatism, then Scientist A does; but the critic then points out that Scientist A does not test a certain hypothesis in this way, and concludes that the empirical, descriptive version of holistic pragmatism is false. Thus the critic forces the holistic pragmatist to deny the descriptive version of his thesis by using that very thesis in refuting it by means of a counterexample, so that the holistic pragmatist who views his thesis descriptively and empirically is hoist with his own petard. How should he respond?

I think the holistic pragmatist should say in reply that *some* logical principles are immune to rejection by experience—namely, those involved in the holistic pragmatist's hypothetico-deductive method of testing—and that the doctrine of holistic pragmatism is also immune to rejection by experience because the holistic pragmatist resolves to hold on to it. This implies that the Duhemian conjunction or scientific heritage of each scientist or scientifically oriented thinker contains two kinds of statements: those that they resolve to immunize against refutation by experience, and those that they do not resolve to immunize. Consequently, as I have argued elsewhere,[1] the holistic pragmatist's heritage is heterogeneous in composition: it may contain logical statements, epistemological statements, physical statements, and even moral principles. The holistic pragmatist may *begin* by asserting something empirical about the testing behavior of scientists—at which point his thesis describes the actual practices or customs of scientists—but when he later rules that no experience *may* disconfirm holistic pragmatism, he behaves somewhat as a legislator does when transforming a custom into a law. The holistic pragmatist transforms his description of how scientists *do* support beliefs into a rule or convention that they *should* follow in testing their beliefs, thereby protecting it from refutation by a putative counterexample of the kind proposed by the critic of holistic pragmatism who treats it as an empirical, descriptive hypothesis.

The holistic pragmatist's transformation of an empirical statement into a normative statement or rule is the counterpart of what a physicist does when transforming a universal empirical statement about iron into a definition of "iron". The physicist may learn empirically that all things she initially calls iron are identifiable by means of different constants—for example, by iron's stretch modulus, by its coefficient of linear expansion, and by its specific heat—but later she may decide to define the term "iron" by means of one of them. In that case she converts an empirically established physical

---

[1] See my *Toward Reunion in Philosophy* (Cambridge, Mass., 1956), pp. 287–88.

truth into a rule that defines "iron", whereas an epistemologist who first says that in fact all and only scientists test their theories in the manner described by his holistic pragmatism converts his empirical statement about a custom of scientists into a rule that defines "scientist" so as to protect his thesis against his critic.

At this point, just as some philosophers may argue that the constant referred to in the definition of "iron" is one that expresses the essence of iron or the meaning of the word "iron", so they may argue that the feature of science which is presented in the *rule* of holistic pragmatism is the essence of science or the meaning of the word "science". Underlying this view is the idea that the definitional rule of holistic pragmatism can be supported only by suprascientific philosophical insight into meanings, whereas the view I adopt is one that Dewey espoused when he was not making his dubious distinction between existential and ideational statements. He said then that one who elects to engage in science does something like entering into a contract.[2] When a man declares himself to be a scientific thinker, he agrees to behave in a certain way; he agrees to test his beliefs in accordance with, say, holistic pragmatism, and if he does not test them in that way, he violates a rule that governs the office he has accepted. He cannot be forced to be a scientific thinker, but once he elects to become one, he promises or agrees to test his theories in a certain way.

When we regard the thesis of holistic pragmatism as a rule, I think we make sense of the idea that epistemology is a normative discipline. But—and this is crucial—saying that it is a rule does not make it immutable, just as turning a custom into a legal statute does not make the custom or the statute immutable. Its status as a rule instead makes the thesis of holistic pragmatism a principle that is not to be cast off lightly. As the principle of conservation of energy is one that a physicist does not lightly surrender, so the principle of holistic pragmatism is one that a holistic pragmatist does not lightly surren-

---

[2] John Dewey, *Logic: The Theory of Inquiry* (New York, 1938), pp. 16–17.

der. Resolving to accept holistic pragmatism does not mean that it can *never* be altered or surrendered, but it does mean that a very powerful argument would be required to effect either of those changes. The beliefs we turn into rules are thereby pinned down by us, but what is so pinned may later be unpinned. It might be said that these rules are accepted *a priori*; but since a pinned-down belief may cease to be pinned, the pinned down is not coextensive with the *a priori* as conceived by many philosophers. It can be a statement in epistemology, logic, physics, or ethics; it can even be an observation sentence. Sometimes we indicate its pinned-down status by making it a definition, but at other times we indicate that status merely by resolving to hold on to it. However, this is not to say "Once pinned down always pinned down", or that our pinned-down beliefs are established by peering at what Dewey calls antecedent meanings.

By approaching the matter in this way, I think that Rawls might pin down his Kantian principle along with the principles of logic that govern the testing of all Duhemian conjunctions and the principle of holistic pragmatism itself. I see no inconsistency with holistic pragmatism in pinning the Kantian principle down, especially because it would have good company in the principle of holistic pragmatism and in the logical principles used in holistic-pragmatic testing.[3] I suspect that the reason why some philosophers may hesitate to pin down moral principles in this way is that they think they are not analytic; but once they abandon the idea that to be pinned down is to be analytic or true by virtue of meanings, they can see more readily that statements of epistemology, logic, ethics, or physics may be pinned down in this fashion. If it be said that pinned-down statements which are called rules are synthetic *a priori*, my answer is that they differ from traditional synthetic *a priori* statements in not being

---

[3] I have focused on this Kantian principle because when my book *What Is and What Ought to Be Done* appeared in 1981, Rawls told me that he for the most part agreed with what I then called epistemological corporatism rather than holistic pragmatism but added that he had a number of reservations that derived from Kantian themes that he wanted to preserve. These themes are evident throughout *A Theory of Justice*.

necessary or pinned down forever. They are entrenched but they may be removed from their trench for good reason. What I decline to say is that they are entrenched because they are seen to be true by virtue of relations between abstract meanings or by examining essences. Kant said that all knowledge *begins* with experience but he added that *a priori* knowledge is known "on the basis of mere concepts", whereas I maintain that a decision to pin down a statement or view it as a rule does not rest on an examination of concepts, meanings, essences, or ideas.

Since I began this study by presenting James's defense of mysticism, I want to conclude it with a story of his about supporting principles that reveals a side of his thinking I find more congenial. He tells of an "old woman who described the world as resting on a rock, and then explained that rock to be supported by another rock, and finally when pushed with questions said it was rocks all the way down."[4] The old woman's answer is not unlike the answer of those who, in Dewey's phrase, shove meanings under pinned-down principles. And principles that are not pinned down were well characterized by James when he contrasted the absolutist in ethics with her opponent. He said that when the anti-absolutist's feelings are at war with principles, she "is always free to seek harmony by toning down the sensitiveness of the feelings". James added that "truckling, compromise, time-serving, capitulations of conscience, are conventionally opprobrious names for what, if successfully carried out, would be on [the anti-absolutist's] principles by far the easiest and most praiseworthy mode of bringing about . . . harmony[.]" By contrast, James said, the absolute moralist "is not free to gain harmony in this way". According to the absolutist, principles "should be as they are and not otherwise".[5] However, if we acknowledge that there are pinned and unpinned moral statements, pinned and unpinned logical statements, pinned and unpinned epistemological statements,

---

[4] William James, "The Sentiment of Rationality," in *The Will to Believe and Other Essays in Popular Philosophy* (New York, 1898), p. 104.

[5] Ibid., pp. 104–5.

and pinned and unpinned physical statements, we deny that *all* logical statements, *all* moral statements, and *all* physical statements have the same epistemic status. James says that "the most violent revolutions in an individual's belief leave most of his old order standing," and as an example of how loyalty to older truth controls scientific thinking he cites an episode in the history of science: " 'Radium' came the other day . . . and seemed for a moment to contradict our idea of the whole order of nature, that order having come to be identified with what is called conservation of energy. The mere sight of radium paying heat away indefinitely out of its own pocket seemed to violate that conservation. What to think?"[6] James then tells us how the principle of conservation of energy was saved by scientists of his day; but what is philosophically important to note is that in resolving to hold on to it they endowed the principle of conservation of energy with an epistemic status like that of holistic pragmatism itself.

I must add, however, that although James speaks of our loyalty to old truths he does not say that every *old* truth commands our loyalty. Some of them, he says, "may grow stiff with years of veteran service and petrified in men's regard by sheer antiquity,"[7] and though we *resolve* to hold on to some of them, we may later withdraw our resolution. This is in keeping with James's Duhem-like observation that the thinker who learns of a counterexample to his theory seeks to escape his trouble "by modifying his previous mass of opinions. He saves as much of it as he can, for in this matter of belief we are all extreme conservatives. So he tries to change first this opinion, and then that (for they resist change variously)[.]"[8] In my view, the principle of holistic pragmatism resists change in the highest degree, and that is why we resolve to hold on to it. Viewing it in this way helps us see why a holistic pragmatist cannot be refuted by calling

[6] William James, *Pragmatism*, [ed. Fredson Bowers and Ignas K. Skrupskelis] (Cambridge, Mass., 1975), pp. 35, 36.

[7] Ibid., p. 37.

[8] Ibid., p. 35.

attention to a particular scientist's failure to test a theory in accordance with holistic pragmatism. Although the holistic pragmatist presents a definition of scientific testing, we know that a particular person who is called a scientist may fail on occasion to test a theory in accordance with that definition. Moreover, because scientists once used a method of testing that was superseded and therefore required a redefinition of scientific testing, the holistic pragmatist cannot be sure that the method of testing he has called scientific will not change in the future and require another change in its definition. I am unable to say exactly how it will change, but since our ancestors did not predict the advent of the method of holistic pragmatism, I hesitate to argue for the permanency of holistic pragmatism's present definition of scientific testing. Furthermore, as I have said, it does not help to maintain that holistic pragmatists can see that it is the essence of science to behave in accordance with their view. Even if one holds that the goal, rather than the essence, of science is to predict, that goal may be more effectively reached in the future by a method that is different from the one now prescribed by holistic pragmatism.

I must add, however, that the holistic pragmatist does not promulgate his definitional rule arbitrarily: he bases it partly on a belief that scientists customarily operate in accordance with his rule and partly on a belief that operating in accordance with it has advantages like those of any good definition. This corresponds to what legislators do when converting a custom into a rule, since the holistic pragmatist who regards his definition as a rule thinks that using it will benefit scientific thinking and speaking. This suggests that some philosophers may concentrate on the customs of scientific thinking, for those who do so help the philosophical legislator see what rules should be created. By describing prevailing customs, they help the philosophical legislator as the anthropologist or sociologist may help the legal legislator.

In this study I have maintained that thinkers who seek knowledge do and should use the method of holistic pragmatism in testing their views, and therefore that theorists of art, moral thinkers, historians, political thinkers, and predicting lawyers do and should. Moreover, even if one thinks that art and religion are not exclusively cognitive, philosophers of art and religion do and should use the method of holistic pragmatism when inquiring into them—especially philosophers who are willing to learn from the behavioral sciences and biology as James, Dewey, and Quine were.

Philosophy is in great measure what philosophers do, just as language is what people speak, and it is not helpful to identify philosophy by means of slogans such as "Philosophy is nothing but the logical analysis of science", when "science" denotes a very limited class of disciplines. Philosophy is an institution with a very long history and is therefore like language, of which John Stuart Mill once wrote: "Language, as Sir James Mackintosh used to say of governments, 'is not made, but grows.' A name is not imposed at once and by previous purpose upon a *class* of objects, but is first applied to one thing, and then extended by a series of transitions to another and another". Immediately after this, and about a century before Wittgenstein's similar remarks on games, Mill said that "a name not unfrequently passes by successive links of resemblance from one object to another, until it becomes applied to things having nothing in common with the first things to which the name was given; which, however, do not, for that reason, drop the name".[9]

Like Mill, and like Wittgenstein when he said that games are linked by what he called a family resemblance instead of by one attribute, I believe that the word "philosophy" also refers to a family of problems. I also want to credit Mill with saying something similar to my statement that philosophers may, after empirically discovering that scientists customarily use the method of holistic pragmatism, turn holistic pragmatism into a rule or a definition of the Wittgen-

[9] John Stuart Mill, *A System of Logic, Ratiocinative and Inductive: Being a Connected View of the Principles of Evidence, and the Methods of Scientific Investigation*, ed. J. M. Robson (Toronto, 1973), book I, chap. 8, sec. 7 (1:151–52). See also Ludwig Wittgenstein, *Philosophical Investigations*, trans. G. E. M. Anscombe (Oxford, 1978), sec. 67 (p. 32).

steinian language-game of science. Mill wrote "that the study of the spontaneous growth of languages is of the utmost importance to those who would logically remodel them. The classifications rudely made by established language, when retouched, as they almost all require to be, by the hands of the logician, are often in themselves excellently suited to his purposes. As compared with the classifications of a philosopher, they are like the customary law of a country, which has grown up as it were spontaneously, compared with laws methodized and digested into a code."[10] In my view, a philosopher may not only study what Mill called established language—the analogue of Mill's customary law—but also remodel it. That also applies to the remodeling of holistic pragmatism when we call it a rule or definition of scientific testing in order to protect it from the objections that face a purely descriptive interpretation of it.

After reading this, some may wonder whether I have committed the sin of epistemic dualism against which I have inveighed so much. For have I not distinguished between a rule and an empirical statement, and is that distinction not as objectionable as the sharp distinction between the analytic and the synthetic as well as that between the *a priori* and the *a posteriori*? Of this sin I believe I am not guilty, for a reason that I repeat: a rule, like a legal statute, is not immutable, since changes in the institution of scientific thinking require its rules to change as changes in customs require the laws of a country to change. Therefore, the rule of holistic pragmatism differs from the analytic, *a priori*, necessary, and self-evident truths that classical rationalists such as Descartes and half-rationalists such as Hume accept. And so long as this rule is regarded as mutable, it is not separated from empirical beliefs by the epistemic chasm that rationalism creates.

Some philosophers might feel uneasy about being relieved of the job of analyzing attributes or essences in a manner that supposedly distinguishes philosophy from physics; they might complain while

---

[10] Mill, *Logic*, book I, chap. 8, sec. 7 (1:153).

seeking to differentiate their product that physicists also propose definitional rules and assert empirical truths. But philosophers seeking a distinctive role should not fear this resemblance of philosophy to physics, since philosophers promulgate definitions of "science" rather than definitions of "iron" and they describe the uses of language rather than the behavior of particles. One philosophical task is that of the descriptive epistemologist, whereas the other is that of the normative epistemologist; the latter should welcome the cooperation of the former, who describes customs and thereby facilitates the latter's construction of definition and rules. In my opinion this pair of tasks is likely to be more rewarding than trying to analyze occult essences or meanings, and philosophers who avoid those blind alleys of rationalism may even come to believe that philosophy of culture is philosophy enough.

Index